家常100

FAVORITE CHINESE DISHES

作　　者　林麗華
編　著　者　財團法人味全文化教育基金會
烹飪製作　味全家政班
翻　　譯　華康妮・黃麗莎
攝　　影　江文榮
印　　刷　中華彩色印刷股份有限公司
出　版　者　純青出版社有限公司
　　　　　台北市松江路125號5樓
　　　　　郵政劃撥1210629－9
　　　　　電話：（02）507－4902・508－4331
總　經　銷　味全出版社有限公司
　　　　　台北市仁愛路4段28號2樓
　　　　　電話：（02）702－1148・702－1149
版權所有　局版台業字第3884號
　　　　　中華民國81年1月初版
定　　價　新台幣貳佰伍拾元整

Author	Lee Hwa Lin
Editor	Wei-Chuan Cultural-Educational Foundation
Dishes prepared by	The Cooking School of the Wei-Chuan Cultural-Educational Foundation
English translation	Connie Wolhardt, Elizabeth Huang
Photography	Williams Chiang
Production	China Color Printing Co., Inc.
Publisher	Chin Chin Publishing co., Ltd.
	5th fl., 125, Sung Chiang Rd, Taipei, Taiwan, R.O.C.
	TEL: (02) 507-4902 . 508-4331
Distributor	Wei-Chuan Publishing co., Ltd.
	2nd fl, 28 Sec.4. Jen-Ai Road, Taipei, Taiwan.
	TEL: (02) 702-1148 . 702-1149
	Wei-Chuan's Publishing
	1455 Monterey Pass Rd, #110
	Monterey Park, CA 91754, U.S.A.
	Tel: (213) 261-3880 . 261-3878
Copyright	1992 by Lee Hwa Lin
	All rights reserved
	First Printing, January, 1992
	ISBN 0-941676-27-7

序

　　自民國七十四年味全文教基金會推出中文版「家常菜」一書以來，深受讀者喜好，已多次再版。因此筆者將近年來味全家政班老師上課所教的菜，挑出一百道家常口味，將其作法簡單化，集結成書。

　　筆者旅居國外數年，深知在國外要買中國菜的材料不易，加上做菜手續繁瑣，不但外國人，甚至中國人都認為烹調中國菜是很費功夫的。針對這點，為了使大家能喜歡做中國菜，我們精選的一百道菜餚，其材料不但在國內一般超級市場容易買到，甚至在國外東方雜貨店或一般有東方材料部門的超級市場均可買到。

　　烹飪原不是一件複雜的工作，較困難的是如何把生鮮食品變成可口好吃的菜餚，其要訣除了材料的選擇及調味料的調配外，火候的大小及做菜前的處理也是很重要的。火候的大小雖然可以憑個人經驗揣摩出來；但是對初學者或不常做菜的讀者未必會掌握箇中三昧，因此本書特別介紹大火、中火、小火的使用狀態，同時區別七分熱與八分熱的油溫，以供讀者參考。另外，對於常常用到或較難處理的材料，我們更特別用圖片簡單示範前處理的工作，以俾讀者能收到事半功倍之效，也是本書的特色之一。

　　這本書能順利推出，除了感謝基金會全體同仁的努力外，也謝謝味全食譜的讀者多年來給我們的支持與鼓勵，我們會一秉初衷，製作企劃更多的好食譜，以饗讀者。

FOREWORD

The Chinese language edition of Chinese Everyday Cooking, published by the Wei-Chuan cultural-Educational Foundation in 1985, was extremely well received by our readers, and has been through several reprintings. In response to this favorable reception, I have selected and simplified 100 of the dishes taught in Wei-Chuan's cooking classes and compiled them into this cookbook.

Having lived abroad for a number of years, I am well aware of how it can sometimes be difficult to obtain the ingredients needed in Chinese cooking. Also, the procedures involved in making some of the dishes can be complex and time-consuming. This can be as frustrating to a native Chinese as to someone who is new to the world of Chinese cuisine. In order to enable anyone and everyone to enjoy the pleasures of delicious Chinese home cooking, the 100 dishes featured in this book can be made with ingredients easily available in Oriental groceries and Oriental specialty departments of supermarkets in English-speaking countries.

Cooking does not have to be complicated. Probably the two most crucial tasks after selecting the right ingredients and seasonings are preparation of the ingredients before cooking and controlling the heat source. For beginners who don't have the experience to draw on that a seasoned cook does, this book features a special reference section explaining the three main levels of cooking heat—high, medium, and low—and the uses of each one. Also, the heat of cooking oil is graded on a scale of one to ten, and the difference between levels seven and eight (two frequently used heat levels) is clearly described. To save the reader time and guesswork, this book offers full, clear illustrations of basic preparation procedures and ones difficult to describe in words.

We are grateful to all of our colleagues at the Wei-Chuan Cultural-Educational Foundation for their tireless contributions to this volume. We also thank you, our readers for your years of support and encouragement. We pledge to continue serving you in the future with even more and better creative cooking ideas.

Lee Hwa Lin

重量換算表
Measure Equivalents

600克＝1斤＝1.32磅
1斤＝16兩
1磅＝16盎士

600 g. = 1 catty = 1.32 1b.
1 catty = 16 taels
1 1b. = 16 oz.

火候的用法
Heat Equivalents

6分熱油約爲120°C或248°F
7分熱油約爲140°C或284°F
8分熱油約爲160°C或320°F

60% hot oil is approximately 120°C or 248°F
70% hot oil is approximately 140°C or 284°F
80% hot oil is approximately 160°C or 320°F

　　火候在中國菜的烹調上佔著相當重要的份量，也唯有火候應用得當，方可展現中國菜的精華，因此，如何妥善掌握住火候，便成爲烹調能否成功的關鍵。大中小火的說明約如下：

　　一般的瓦斯爐台，有大、中、小火或前段、中段、後段火之區分，有的甚至沒有標示；其實，所謂的大火是指開到最大極限之火力，通常用於煮開羹湯或蒸或快炒蔬菜等，要在短時間內烹調菜餚。中火即中度火力，是爲使食物完全熟透且酥脆，並不至燒焦的某一固定溫度範圍。小火是指最小之火力，通常用於已煮開之羹湯要維持沸騰或燉煮不易熟爛之肉類而需較長烹調時間時用之。

　　Heat occupies an important position in Chinese cooking. Only when the heat is controlled correctly, can the essence of Chinese cooking emerge. Therefore, this book devoted this page especially to explain heat.

　　Generally, there are high, medium, low heat or 1, 2, 3 sections on our gas stoves; some even do not have any indications at all. Socalled high heat means turn on the heat to the maximum extent; usually used for bringing soup to boil, to steam, to stir fry vegetables, or for quick cooking dishes. Medium heat means turn on the heat to the medium extent. It remains at a steady temperature for thorough cooking and crispy for frying; at the same time does not risk burning. Low heat means the minimum heat, generally used for simmering already boiled soup or stewing dishes, which require a rather long cooking time.

材料的前處理
Glossaries and Preparation of Special Food Materials

蚵的清洗
Oysters

❶加太白粉、鹽於蚵中。
❷輕輕拌勻。
❸用清水沖洗乾淨即可。

❶ Add corn starch and salt into the oysters.
❷ Mix gently.
❸ Rinse clean with water.

蟹的清洗方法
Crabs

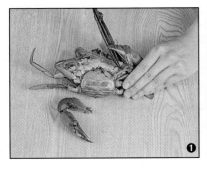

❶將蟹的大螯剪斷。
❷蟹外殼洗刷乾淨。
❸掀起殼蓋，去掉蓋內之腸泥及蟹身上之鰓即可。

❶ Snip off the big claws.
❷ Brush clean the outer shells.
❸ Pull off the top shell, clean the inner shell and discard the gills.

薑酒汁作法
Ginger Wine

❶薑30公克磨碎。
❷加酒1大匙。
❸瀝出之湯汁即爲薑酒汁。

❶ Mince 30 g. of ginger.
❷ Add 1 T. of cooking wine.
❸ Drain out the juice, which is called ginger wine.

高湯作法
Stock

❶以豬、牛、雞的肉或骨頭入開水中川燙。
❷再將肉或骨頭取出洗淨。
❸將水燒開，再入肉或骨頭，並加少許葱、薑、酒，慢
　火熬煮出來的湯，謂之高湯。

❶ Parboil pork, beef, chicken or bones in boiling water.
❷ Life out and wash clean.
❸ Bring new water to boil, add in meat or bones; then add a little green onion, ginger and cooking wine. Cook slowly over simmering heat until the soup is tasty. Strain for use.

葱段的處理
Green Onion Sections

❶將葱洗淨。
❷去頭、尾部份。
❸切成3公分長段。

❶ Wash the green onions.
❷ Trim off the top parts and roots.
❸ Cut into 3 cm (1¹/₃") long sections.

牛肉的切法
Sliced Beef

❶將牛里肌肉洗淨。
❷放入冰庫中至半結凍狀態再取出。
❸逆紋切斜片。

❶ Wash the beef tenderloin.
❷ Put the beef in the freezer until half frozen.
❸ Cut into slanting slices against the grains.

乾木耳的處理
Dried Wood Ears

❶乾木耳用水泡軟。

❷洗淨。

❸去蒂。

❶ Soak the wood ears until softened.

❷ Wash clean.

❸ Cut off the stems.

蛤蜊的處理方法
Clams

❶以水1杯加鹽1小匙的比例，調到鹽溶解。

❷倒入盛有蛤蜊的容器內，水不必淹蓋過蛤蜊，置數小時，待吐沙後即可使用。

❶ Add 1 t. of salt for each cup of water; mix until the salt has dissolved.

❷ Pour over the clams, the solution does not need to cover the clams completely. Let it stand for a few hours until the clams have "spit-out" all the sand.

發海參的方法
Dried Sea Cucumber

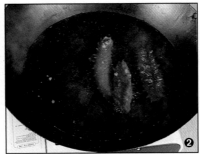

❶海參洗淨，泡水一天。

❷隔天換水煮開後熄火，待水涼後換水，再煮開；如此
一天3次，連續發2天至軟。

❸由腹部剪開，取出內臟洗淨，加水煮開再發1天，即可
使用。

❶ Wash the dried sea cucumber, soak in water for
one day.

❷ Change the sea cucumber into new water the
next day and bring the water to one boil. When
the water is cooled, change again to new water;
bring to boil again. Repeat the process 3 times a
day for 2 days until the sea cucumber has
softened.

❸ Snip open lengthwise and clean out the intestines.
Cover the sea cucumber with cold water and
bring it to boil. Remove from heat and let it stand
for one day.

薑片的處理
Sliced Ginger

❶薑洗淨去皮。

❷切片。

❶ Wash and skin the ginger.

❷ Cut into slices.

烹調的方法
Guide to Cooking Terms

熱菜
Stir Fry

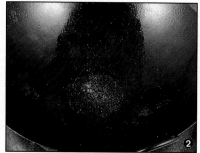

❶先熱鍋。

❷入油後再加熱。

❸入葱、薑、蒜……等爆炒至香味出來。

❹入食物後以大火快速翻炒，避免沾鍋。

❶ Heat the wok.

❷ Add oil and heat again.

❸ Add green onion, ginger, garlic or other ingredients; fry until the fragances of the ingredients arise.

❹ When the ingredients are added, they should be stirred quickly over high heat and should avoid sticking to the wok.

川燙
Blanch

❶水以大火煮沸。
❷放入材料快煮，隨即撈起。
❸漂冷水。

❶ Bring water to boil over high heat.
❷ Add in the ingredients; boil slightly and quickly life out.
❸ Rinse under cold water.

過油
Hot Oil Soaking

❶將食物泡入熱油內（6分熱，120℃），食物剛熟即刻撈出，時間不可過長，謂之過油。

❶ Soak the food into hot oil (60% hot, 120℃), lift out as soon as the food is cooked. It should be done in a minimum of time.

目錄 Contents

6人份 Serves 6

涼拌花枝(圖左 illus. left)
Squid in Garlic Sauce

花枝⋯⋯⋯⋯⋯⋯300公克
西芹⋯⋯⋯⋯⋯⋯150公克
紅辣椒絲⋯⋯⋯⋯⋯1大匙

① 醬油⋯⋯⋯⋯⋯1½大匙
　蒜泥、麻油⋯⋯各1大匙
　糖、白醋⋯⋯⋯各1小匙
　黑醋⋯⋯⋯⋯⋯少許

❶ 花枝洗淨切細絲；西芹洗淨去老纖維，亦切細絲備用。
❷ 水煮開，先入西芹燙熟，取出以冰開水漂涼，瀝乾置盤；再入花枝燙熟，取出以冰開水漂涼，瀝乾水分，置西芹上；將①料拌勻，淋在花枝上，再撒上紅辣椒絲即可。

■ 也可用蘆筍代替西芹。

300 g. (²/₃ lb.)　squid (remove heads and foreign matter)
150 g. (¹/₃ lb.)　celery
1 T.　　　　　shredded red hot pepper

① 1½ T.　　soy sauce
　1 T. each　mashed garlic, sesame oil
　1 t. each　sugar, white vinegar
　Dash　　black vinegar

❶ Clean and shred the squid. Remove the fibers from the surface of celery, then cut it into small lengths.
❷ Parboil the celery until cooked. Remove and immerse them in ice water. Drain and arrange them on platter. Blanch the squid in boiling water, remove when cooked. Dip in ice water then drain. Place on top of the celery. Pour mixture ① on the squid. Sprinkle with red hot pepper.

■ Asparagus may be used instead of celery.

葱薑爆蟹 (圖上 illus. up)
Crab with Ginger and Onion

❶ 螃蟹處理乾淨後切大塊（參考第5頁），沾太白粉備用。
❷ 鍋熱入油4杯，將螃蟹炸至七分熟撈出；鍋內留油2大匙爆香葱、薑，隨入蟹塊及①料，將蟹塊煮熟後以②料勾芡，最後淋上麻油即可。

❶ Clean the crabs and cut it into large pieces (see page 5), dip into corn starch.
❷ Heat 4 c. of oil in the wok. Deep fry the crabs until almost cooked; remove. Retain 2 T. of oil in the wok. Stir fry the onion and ginger until fragrant. Add the crabs and ①, thicken with ② when cooked. Sprinkle the sesame oil on top of the crabs and serve.

螃蟹······2隻
葱段······12段
薑片······12片
太白粉······3大匙
麻油······1小匙

①
水······½杯
酒······1大匙
醬油、蠔油······各½大匙
鹽······1／8小匙
味精、胡椒粉······各少許

② 水、太白粉······各½大匙

2	crabs
12 sections	green onion
12 slices	ginger
3 T.	corn starch
1 t.	sesame oil

①
½ c.	water
1 T.	cooking wine
½ T. each	soy sauce, oyster sauce
⅛ t.	salt
Dash	pepper

② ½ T. each water, corn starch

鹽酥蝦 (圖右下 illus. right down)
Shell Shrimp with Seasoned Salt

❶ 鱸蝦剪除鬚爪，去腸泥，洗淨瀝乾，加①料拌勻，醃約20分鐘備用。
❷ 油3杯燒至8分熱（約160℃，320℉），將鱸蝦用大火炸約1分半鐘撈出。留油1小匙、炒香②料再放鱸蝦拌勻即可。

■ 家庭小菜可改用新鮮紅蝦或河蝦。

❶ Cut off the antennae and all appendages from the shrimp. Devein and rinse; drain. Marinate in ① for 20 minutes.
❷ Heat 3 c. of oil until it is 320°F (160°C). Deep fry the shrimp for 1 1/2 minutes or until the shell is crispy; remove and drain. Retain 1 t. of oil in the wok, stir fry ② then add shrimp quickly to mix. Serve.

鱸蝦······300公克

①
太白粉······½大匙
薑酒汁······1小匙

②
蒜末······2大匙
紅辣椒末······½大匙
鹽······1小匙
味精······½小匙

300 g. (⅔ 1b.) fresh shrimp with shell

①
| ½ T. | corn starch |
| 1 t. | ginger wine (see page 6) |

②
2 T.	minced garlic
½ T.	minced red hot pepper
1 t.	salt

三色蝦仁
Tri-Colored shrimp

蝦仁、罐頭玉米粒⋯⋯各200公克
青豆仁（冷凍）⋯⋯⋯⋯75公克
薑片⋯⋯⋯⋯⋯⋯⋯⋯⋯⋯2片
① { 酒⋯⋯⋯⋯⋯⋯⋯⋯1小匙
　　 鹽、太白粉⋯⋯⋯各¼小匙
② { 水⋯⋯⋯⋯⋯⋯⋯⋯2大匙
　　 鹽、味精⋯⋯⋯⋯各1小匙
　　 太白粉⋯⋯⋯⋯⋯⋯½小匙
　　 酒、胡椒粉⋯⋯⋯各少許

200 g. (7 oz.) each shelled shrimps,
　　　　　　　　　canned or
　　　　　　　　　frozen corn
75 g. (2½ oz.)　　frozen green
　　　　　　　　　peas
2 slices　　　　　ginger
① { 1 t.　　　　cooking wine
　　 ¼ t. each　salt,
　　　　　　　　corn starch
② { 2 T.　　　　water
　　 1 t.　　　　salt
　　 ½ t.　　　　corn starch
　　 Dash each　cooking wine,
　　　　　　　　pepper

沙拉大蝦
Fried Prawns with Salad Dressing

大蝦⋯⋯⋯⋯⋯⋯12隻
太白粉⋯⋯⋯⋯⋯少許
① { 蛋白⋯⋯⋯⋯1個
　　 酒⋯⋯⋯⋯⋯1小匙
　　 鹽⋯⋯⋯⋯⋯¼小匙
　　 胡椒粉⋯⋯⋯少許
② { 奶水⋯⋯⋯6大匙
　　 沙拉醬⋯⋯3大匙

12　　　prawns
Dash　corn starch
① { 1　　　egg white
　　 1 t.　cooking wine
　　 ¼ t.　salt
　　 Dash　pepper
② { 6 T.　milk
　　 3 T.　mayonnaise

❶ 蝦仁去腸泥、洗淨，拭乾水分，以①料醃10分鐘備用。
❷ 鍋熱入油1杯，待熱，入蝦仁至顏色變白，撈出瀝油；鍋內留油2大匙，爆香薑片，入玉米粒、青豆仁炒1分鐘，再放入蝦仁及②料大火快炒均勻即可。

❶ Rinse and devein shrimp; drain. Marinate in ① about 10 minutes.
❷ Heat the wok, then add 1 c. of oil. Fry the shrimps over medium heat until the shrimps' color turns to pale, remove and drain. Retain 2 T. of oil in the wok. Stir fry the ginger until fragrant. Add corn and peas, stir fry about 1 minute. Add shrimps and ②, turn heat to high, and quickly stir fry until well mixed. Serve.

6人份 Serves 6

6人份 Serves 6

❶ 蝦去殼及腸泥，洗淨，拭乾水分，在蝦背部以刀劃開，以①料醃5分鐘，再沾太白粉備用。油3杯燒至140℃（280℉），入蝦以中火炸至金黃色撈出備用。
❷ 鍋內留油1大匙，入炸好的蝦及②料拌勻即可。

❶ Shell the prawns and devein, clean and drain them. Score the back of the prawns to Marinate in ① for 5 minutes, then dip them in the corn starch. Heat 3 c. of oil up to 280°F (140℃). Deep fry the prawns over medium heat until their color turns to golden brown; remove and drain.

桂花魚翅
Fried Shark's Fin with Vegetable

魚翅（已發好的如圖1）……180公克
里肌肉……………………………100公克
雞蛋…………………………………4個
香菇…………………………………3朵
筍絲、洋蔥絲………………………各100公克
熟紅蘿蔔絲…………………………50公克

① 醬油………½大匙
　 太白粉……1小匙
　 酒…………½小匙

② 水……………1大匙
　 糖……………½小匙
　 鹽、味精…………各¼小匙
　 麻油、胡椒粉……各少許

180 g. (6½ oz.)
　　presoftened shark's fin (illus. 1)
100 g. (3½ oz.)　　lean pork
4　　eggs
3　　dried black mushrooms
100 g. (3½ oz.) each
　　shredded bamboo shoots,
　　shredded onions
50 g. (1¾ oz.)
　　shredded precooked carrots

① ½ T.　soy sauce
　 1 t.　corn starch
　 ½ t.　cooking wine

② 1 T.　　　water
　 ½ t.　　　sugar
　 ¼ t.　　　salt
　 Dash each　sesame oil, pepper

❶ 魚翅用開水燙過瀝乾，香菇泡軟去蒂切絲（圖2）備用；里肌肉切絲入①料拌勻。
❷ 鍋熱入油2大匙，炒熟肉絲撈起，餘油炒熟洋蔥絲，均備用。
❸ 雞蛋打散，入香菇絲、筍絲、紅蘿蔔絲、洋蔥絲及②料。
❹ 鍋熱入油2大匙，待熱入❸項材料拌炒數下後，入魚翅及里肌肉拌炒至熟即可。

❶ Parboil the shark's fin and drain. Soak the mushrooms in warm water until softened ; remove the stems and cut into julienne strips (illus. 2). Shred the lean pork and mix in ①.
❷ Heat the wok, then add 2 T. of oil, stir fry the pork until cooked; remove. Reheat the remaining oil in the wok, fry the onion until cooked; remove.
❸ Beat the egg lightly, mix in the mushrooms, bamboo shoots, carrots, onions and ② for later use.
❹ Heat the wok, then add 2 T. of oil. Quickly stir in and mix the ingredients of paragraph 3 above. Add the shark's fin and pork, fry until cooked, then serve.

芹菜魷魚
Squid with Celery

鮮魷魚·····················370公克
芹菜·······················300公克
薑絲························1大匙
紅辣椒絲····················½小匙
蔥段·······················8段

① 水·······················4大匙
　 鹽、糖、酒、醋······各1小匙
　 太白粉····················½小匙
　 味精······················¼小匙
　 胡椒粉····················少許

370 g. (13 oz.)
　　squid (body part only)

300 g. (²/₃ lb.)　celery
1 T.　　　　shredded ginger
½ t.　　　　shredded red
　　　　　　hot pepper
8 sections　green onion
① 4 T.　　　water
　 1 t. each　salt, sugar,
　　　　　　cooking wine, vinegar
　 ½ t.　　　corn starch
　 Dash　　pepper

❶ 魷魚洗淨切花(圖1)，以開水燙至捲起即撈出(圖2)，瀝乾水分；芹菜洗淨，去老纖維，切4公分長段備用。
❷ 鍋熱入油3大匙，續入蔥段、薑絲及紅辣椒絲炒香，再放芹菜、魷魚及①料拌炒數下即可。

❶ Clean the squid. Score the inside surface lengthwise and crosswise (illus.1), then cut the squid into pieces. Blanch in boiling water until they curl (illus.2); remove and drain. Wash the celery and remove the fibers from surface. Cut it into 4 cm (1⁴/₅") pieces.
❷ Heat the wok, then add 3 T. of oil. Stir fry the onion, ginger and hot red pepper until fragrant. Add the celery, squid and ①, stir quickly; remove and serve.

鮮蚵草菇
Oyster with Straw Mushrooms

蚵⋯⋯⋯⋯⋯⋯⋯⋯220公克
青江菜（圖1）⋯⋯⋯300公克
草菇⋯⋯⋯⋯⋯⋯⋯⋯200公克
酒⋯⋯⋯⋯⋯⋯⋯⋯⋯1大匙

① { 葱白⋯⋯⋯⋯⋯6段
　　蒜末、薑末⋯⋯各1大匙

② { 酒⋯⋯⋯⋯⋯⋯½大匙
　　鹽⋯⋯⋯⋯⋯⋯½小匙

③ { 水⋯⋯⋯⋯⋯⋯⋯1杯
　　酒、醬油⋯⋯⋯各2大匙
　　鹽、糖⋯⋯⋯⋯各1小匙
　　胡椒粉⋯⋯⋯⋯½小匙

④ 水、太白粉⋯⋯⋯各1大匙

200 g. (½ lb.)　oyster
300 g. (⅔ lb.)　bok choy (illus. 1)
200 g. (½ lb.)　straw mushrooms
1 T.　　　　　　cooking wine
① { 6 sections　green onion
　　　　　　　　(white section only)
　　1 T. each　minced garlic,
　　　　　　　　minced ginger
② { ½ T.　cooking wine
　　½ t.　salt
③ { 1 c.　　　　water
　　2 T. each　cooking wine,
　　　　　　　　soy sauce
　　1 t. each　salt, sugar
　　½ t.　　　　pepper
④ 1 T. each　water, corn starch

❶ 鍋熱入油1大匙，將青江菜加②料炒至9分熟，取出排盤圍邊，多餘的放在盤中央墊底備用。
❷ 草菇對切，入滾水中煮2分鐘，撈出、漂涼、瀝乾，生蚵洗淨均備用（參考第5頁）。
❸ 鍋熱入油1大匙，爆香①料，入生蚵拌炒數下，續入③料煮開，撈出蚵後再入草菇及酒煮開，改小火煮至汁剩1杯，以④料勾芡再加蚵拌勻，撈起置盤中央即可。

❶ Heat the wok, then add 1 T. of oil. Stir fry the bok choy and ②. When cooked, remove and arrange on a serving platter.
❷ Cut the straw mushrooms in half. Parboil in water for 2 minutes; remove and drain. Wash the oyster. (see page 5 for basic preparation)
❸ Heat the wok, then add 1 T. of oil. Fry ① until fragrant, then add the oyster and stir briefly. Add ③ bring it to a boil; remove the oyster, then add the straw mushrooms and wine. Bring them to a boil then turn the heat to low, cook until the liquid is reduced to 1 c. Add ④ to thicken and return the oyster to the wok; blend well. Pour them on the center of the platter and serve.

魚香鮮貝
Scallops a La Szechwan

鮮貝	·················	300公克
草菇	·················	6個
小黃瓜	·················	12片

① 葱末·················3大匙
　薑末、蒜末·········各1大匙
　辣椒醬·················½小匙

② 酒、太白粉·········各½大匙
　鹽·················¼小匙

③ 水·················3大匙
　酒、糖、醋、醬油······各½大匙
　麻油、太白粉··········各1小匙
　鹽·················⅓小匙

300 g. (²/₃ 1b.)	scallops
6	straw mushrooms
12 slices	gherkin cucumber

① 3 T. minced green onion
　1 T. each minced ginger, minced garlic
　½ t. hot pepper sauce

② ½ T. each cooking wine, corn starch
　¼ t. salt

③ 3 T. water
　½ T. each cooking wine, sugar, vinegar, soy sauce
　1 t. each sesame oil, corn starch
　⅓ t. salt

❶ 鮮貝橫切片，入②料醃30分鐘；草菇對切（圖1）備用。
❷ 鍋熱入油1杯燒熱，入鮮貝泡熟撈出。留油2大匙炒香①料，再入草菇、小黃瓜略炒，最後入鮮貝及③料拌勻即可

❶ Slice the scallops cross-wise, marinate in ② about 30 minutes. Lengthwise, halve the mushrooms (illus. 1).
❷ Heat the wok, then add 1 c. of oil. Fry the scallops over medium heat until cooked, remove and drain. Retain 2 T. of oil, stir fry ① until fragrant. Add mushrooms and cucumbers, stir fry for few minutes. Add scallops and ③ turn heat to high, and quickly stir fry, remove and serve.

蘆筍鮮貝
Scallops with Asparagus

6人份 Serves 6

鮮貝、綠蘆筍…………各300公克
熟紅蘿蔔片……………6片
酒………………………1大匙

① {
葱段………………6段
薑片………………6片
紅辣椒片…………1大匙
蒜末………………1小匙
}

② {
酒、太白粉………各½大匙
鹽…………………¼小匙
}

③ {
水…………………2大匙
麻油、太白粉……各1小匙
鹽…………………⅓小匙
味精、胡椒粉……各少許
}

0 g. (²/₃ lb.) each scallops,
                    asparagus
slices   precooked carrot
T.   cooking wine

{ 6 sections green onion
  6 slices   ginger
  1 T.   red hot pepper
  1 t.   minced garlic

{ ½ T. each   cooking wine, corn starch
  ¼ t.   salt

{ 2 T.   water
  1 t. each   sesame oil, corn starch
  ⅓ t.   salt
  Dash   pepper

❶ 鮮貝橫切片（圖1）加入②料醃30分鐘；蘆筍切除硬莖及老皮，洗淨切斜段備用。

❷ 鍋熱入油1杯燒熱，入鮮貝泡熟撈出。留油2大匙，先炒香①料，隨入蘆筍並加酒1大匙炒2分鐘後，入鮮貝、熟紅蘿蔔片及③料拌勻即可。

❶ Cut the scallops crosswise in half (illus. 1), marinate them in ② for 30 minutes. Cut off the tough portions of the asparagus; wash them and cut into long strips.

❷ Heat the wok, then add 1 c. of oil. Fry the scallops until cooked; remove. Retain 2 T. of oil in the wok, stir fry ① until fragrant. Add the asparagus and cooking wine and fry for 2 minutes. Finally, mix in the scallops, carrots and ③; stir quickly until thoroughly mixed.

❶

鐵扒魚塊
Stir－Fried Fish Fillets

石斑魚肉‧‧‧‧‧‧‧‧‧‧‧‧‧‧‧‧‧300公克
洋葱絲‧‧‧‧‧‧‧‧‧‧‧‧‧‧‧‧‧‧‧150公克
青豆仁‧‧‧‧‧‧‧‧‧‧‧‧‧‧‧‧‧‧‧2大匙

① { 蛋‧‧‧‧‧‧‧‧‧‧‧‧‧‧‧‧‧‧‧‧½個
太白粉‧‧‧‧‧‧‧‧‧‧‧‧‧‧3大匙
鹽‧‧‧‧‧‧‧‧‧‧‧‧‧‧‧‧‧‧¼小匙
味精、胡椒粉‧‧‧‧‧各少許

② { 水‧‧‧‧‧‧‧‧‧‧‧‧‧‧‧‧‧‧‧‧½杯
白醋‧‧‧‧‧‧‧‧‧‧‧‧‧‧‧‧‧2大匙
糖、蕃茄醬‧‧‧‧‧‧‧各1½大匙
鹽、香酢‧‧‧‧‧‧‧‧‧各½小匙

③ { 水‧‧‧‧‧‧‧‧‧‧‧‧‧‧‧‧‧‧‧‧1大匙
太白粉‧‧‧‧‧‧‧‧‧‧‧‧1½小匙

300 g. (²/₃ 1b.)	fish fillets
150 g. (¹/₃ 1b.)	shredded onions
2 T.	green peas

① {
½	egg
3 T.	corn starch
¼ t.	salt
Dash	pepper

② {
½ c.	water
2 T.	vinegar
1½ T. each	sugar. ketchup
½ t. each	salt, worcestershire sauce

③ {
| 1 T. | water |
| 1½ t. | corn starch |

❶ 石斑魚切片（圖1），入①料拌勻備用。
❷ 鍋熱入油4杯，待熱，入魚片一片片炸熟撈起置盤中。鍋內留油2大匙炒洋葱、青豆仁，再入②料煮沸，以③料勾芡後淋在魚片上即可。

❶ Cut the fish into large, thin slices (illus. 1). Mix thoroughly in ①.
❷ Heat the wok, then add 4 c. of oil. Deep fry the fish. When cooked remove the pieces of fish and place them on a serving platter. Retain 2 T. of oil in the wok, stir fry the onion and green peas, then add ②; bring them to a boil. Thicken with ③ and pour over the fish.

❶

咕咾魚塊
Sweet and Sour Fish Fillets

魚肉‥‥‥‥‥‥‥‥‥‥300公克
洋蔥‥‥‥‥‥‥‥‥‥‥120公克
蔥段‥‥‥‥‥‥‥‥‥‥6段
薑片‥‥‥‥‥‥‥‥‥‥6片

① ┌ 太白粉‥‥‥‥‥‥‥½大匙
　 │ 酒‥‥‥‥‥‥‥‥‥1小匙
　 │ 鹽‥‥‥‥‥‥‥‥‥½小匙
　 └ 麻油、胡椒粉‥‥‥各¼小匙

② ┌ 蕃茄醬‥‥‥‥‥‥‥4大匙
　 │ 糖、醋、水‥‥‥‥各2大匙
　 │ 太白粉‥‥‥‥‥‥‥1小匙
　 └ 鹽‥‥‥‥‥‥‥‥‥¼小匙

300 g. (²/₃ lb.)　fish fillets
120 g. (¹/₄ lb.)　onion
6 sections　　　green onion
6 slices　　　　ginger

① ┌ ½ T.　　　corn starch
　 │ 1 t.　　　cooking wine
　 │ ½ t.　　　salt
　 └ ¼ t. each　sesame oil, pepper

② ┌ 4 T.　　　ketchup
　 │ 2 T. each　sugar, vinegar, water
　 │ 1 t.　　　corn starch
　 └ ¼ t.　　　salt

❶ 魚肉切塊（圖1），入①料拌勻醃約20分鐘；洋蔥切塊備用。
❷ 將3杯油熱至160℃（320°F），以中火將魚肉、洋蔥一起泡熟撈起；鍋內留油1大匙炒香蔥薑，再入②料燒開，續入魚肉及洋蔥炒勻即可。

❶ Cut fish fillets into cubes (illus. 1), mix and marinate in ① for 20 minutes. Cut the onion into same size as the fish.

❷ Heat 3 c. of oil in the wok to 320°F (160°C). Fry the fish and onion over medium heat until cooked; remove and drain. Retain 1 T. of oil in the wok. Stir fry the green onion and ginger until fragrant. Add ②, bring to a boil then add the fish and onion; stir to mix. Remove and serve.

咖哩銀絲蟹
Curry Crabs With Bean Threads

材料：
青蟹…………………………1隻
粉絲…………………………60公克
太白粉………………………3大匙

① { 薑末、蒜末、
碎葱末、青椒末、
紅辣椒末…………各1小匙 }

② { 水…………………………2大匙
咖哩粉…………………½大匙
酒………………………1小匙
糖、鹽…………………各½小匙
味精、胡椒粉……各少許 }

③ { 牛奶……………………½杯
椰漿……………………1大匙
牛油……………………1小匙 }

④ { 水………………………1½小匙
太白粉…………………1小匙 }

1		crab
60 g. (2⅛ oz.)		bean threads
3 T.		corn starch
①	1 t. each	minced ginger, minced garlic, minced green onion, minced green pepper, minced red hot pepper

② { 2 T. — water
½ T. — curry powder
1 t. — cooking wine
½ t. each — sugar, salt
Dash — pepper }

③ { ½ c. — milk
1 T. — coconut milk
1 t. — butter }

④ { 1½ t. — water
1 t. — corn starch }

❶ 青蟹處理乾淨後（圖1），切成6塊，沾太白粉；粉絲以開水泡軟並燙熟、切段。
❷ 鍋熱入油4杯，將青蟹塊炸熟撈出，鍋內留油2大匙爆香①料，入②料炒勻，取一半炒香粉絲，置砂鍋內備用；另一半與蟹塊及③料煮沸，再以④料勾芡，取出置粉絲上。
❸ 食前再將砂鍋燒熱即可。

❶ Clean the crab (illus. 1) and cut it into 6 pieces. Dip the pieces into the corn starch. Boil the bean thread until cooked; remove and cut in half.
❷ Heat 4 c. of oil in the wok. Deep fry the crab until cooked; remove. Retain 2 T. of oil in the wok. Fry ① until fragrant then add ②; and mix well. Remove and divide into two portions. Place one portion of the ingredients in a Chinese clay pot, mix in bean thread and set aside for later use. Mix the other portion of the ingredients with the crabs and ③ in the wok, bring them to a boil. Thicken with ④ pour over on top of bean threads.
❸ Simmer over low heat until the liquid in the pot has almost evaporated and serve.

煙燻黃魚
Smoked Whole Fish

材料：

黃魚‥‥‥‥‥‥‥‥600公克

①
- 葱段‥‥‥‥‥‥‥‥6段
- 薑片‥‥‥‥‥‥‥‥3片
- 八角（圖1）‥‥‥‥2粒
- 水‥‥‥‥‥‥‥‥1½杯
- 酒‥‥‥‥‥‥‥‥1大匙
- 鹽‥‥‥‥‥‥‥‥2小匙

②
- 葱段‥‥‥‥‥‥‥‥6段
- 麵粉‥‥‥‥‥‥‥‥1杯
- 糖‥‥‥‥‥‥‥‥2大匙

③
- 葱末‥‥‥‥‥‥‥‥1大匙
- 麻油‥‥‥‥‥‥‥‥少許

600 g.   yellow fish or whole fish

①
6 sections	green onion
3 slices	ginger
2	star anises (illus. 1)
1½ c.	water
1 T.	cooking wine
2 t.	salt

②
6 sections	green onion
1 c.	flour
2 T.	sugar

③
1 T.	minced green onion
Dash	sesame oil

❶ ①料拌勻，入洗淨的黃魚浸泡30分鐘（中間必須翻面）；鍋熱入油6杯，入黃魚炸熟，撈出備用。

❷ 預熱烤箱至230℃ （450°F），將魚放在上層，下置拌勻之②料，烤約4～5分鐘呈黃色，取出後淋上③料即可。

❶ Mix ① thoroughly and marinate the fish for 30 minutes. (Turn the fish over during marinating.) Heat 6 c. of oil in the wok and deep fry the fish. Remove and drain when it is cooked.

❷ Preheat oven to 450°F (230°C). Put the fish on the greased rack. Mix ② well in a pan, then put it on the bottom rack. Bake the fish for 4 or 5 minutes; remove and sprinkle with ③ and serve.

生煎蝦餅
Fried Shrimp Cakes

6人份 Serves 6

蝦仁⋯⋯⋯⋯⋯⋯180公克
肥肉⋯⋯⋯⋯⋯⋯30公克
葱末⋯⋯⋯⋯⋯⋯2½大匙
薑末、洋火腿末⋯⋯各1大匙
黑芝麻⋯⋯⋯⋯⋯少許
香菜葉⋯⋯⋯⋯⋯12片

① 蛋白⋯⋯⋯1個
太白粉⋯⋯1小匙
鹽⋯⋯⋯⋯¼小匙
味精⋯⋯⋯⅛小匙
胡椒粉⋯⋯少許

② 水⋯⋯⋯⋯2大匙
酒⋯⋯⋯⋯1大匙

180 g. (6⅓ oz.)	shelled shrimp
30 g. (1 oz.)	fat pork
2½ T.	minced green onion
1 T. each	minced ginger, minced ham
12 pieces	coriander leaves
a little	black sesame seeds

① 1 egg white
1 t. corn starch
¼ t. salt
Dash pepper

② 2 T. water
1 T. cooking wine

❶ 黑芝麻及香菜葉均洗淨瀝乾，蝦仁去腸泥（圖1）洗淨，拭乾水分，與肥肉一起剁碎成蝦泥，加葱末、薑末及①料調勻，分成12等份，再用手壓成圓餅狀（圖2），上飾以洋火腿末、黑芝麻及香菜葉是爲蝦餅。
❷ 鍋熱入油2大匙，放入蝦餅，以小火煎熟（約2分鐘），再淋上②料，加燜約2分鐘即可。

■食時可沾花椒鹽或芥末醬味道更佳。

❶ Wash the black sesame seeds and fresh coriander leaves. Devein the shrimp and rinse clean (illus. 1). Pat away the excess moisture with paper towels. Mince the shrimp with the pork into a fine paste. Add the green onion, ginger and ① until thoroughly blended. Press the shrimp mixture into 12 patties(illus.2).Sprinkle a little ham, black sesame seeds, and a coriander leaves onto the top of each patty, pressing them in so that they do not drop off.

❷ Heat the wok, then add 2 T. of oil. Fry shrimp cakes over low heat for 2 minutes or until cooked. Add ②, cover and simmer for another 2 minutes then serve.

■ Pepper and salt mixture or mustard sauce may be used for dipping when served.

脆皮蠣腐捲
Crispy Bean Curd Skin Rolls

蚵·····················225公克
豆腐·····················1塊
豆腐皮····················4張
葱末····················3大匙
麵粉、玉米粉···········各2大匙
①鹽、味精、胡椒粉·····各¼小匙
②水、麵粉················各2大匙

225 g. (8 oz.)	oysters
1	bean curd (tofu)
4 sheets	bean curd skin
3 T.	minced green onion
2 T. each	flour, corn starch
① ¼ t. each	salt, pepper
② 2 T. each	water, flour

❶ 蚵洗淨瀝乾,加玉米粉拌勻;豆腐去水分,以濾網磨細;將蚵、豆腐、葱末及①料拌勻成內餡;②料調勻成麵糊備用。
❷ 豆腐皮每張切成3長條(圖1),上置內餡,再捲成三角形,收口處沾麵糊黏緊(圖2),共做12份備用。
❸ 油6杯,燒至140°C(280°F),入蠣腐捲炸至金黃即可。

■食時可沾胡椒鹽。

❶ Wash the oysters, then drain. Mix them in corn starch. Drain the water from the bean curd, put it through a sieve to make a fine bean curd paste. Mix the oyster, bean curd, green onion and ① together to make the filling. Mix ② to form a paste.
❷ Cut each bean curd skin into 3 long pieces (illus. 1). Spread one portion of the filling on a bean curd sheet, fold to a triangle shape and seal tightly with flour paste (illus. 2). Follow the same procedure with the other 12 rolls.
❸ Heat 6 c. of oil to 280°F (140°C), deep fry the bean curd skin rolls until the color turns to brown and then serve.

■ Pepper and salt mixture may be used for dipping when served.

蘿蔔排骨（圖左 illus. left）
Ribs with Turnip

小排骨‧‧‧‧‧‧‧‧450公克
蘿蔔‧‧‧‧‧‧‧‧‧‧‧300公克
葱段‧‧‧‧‧‧‧‧‧‧‧6段
① 水‧‧‧‧‧‧‧‧2杯
醬油‧‧‧‧‧¼杯
糖‧‧‧‧‧‧‧‧½大匙
鹽‧‧‧‧‧‧‧‧¹/₈小匙

❶ 小排骨切3公分長段，開水川燙備用；蘿蔔去皮，切滾刀塊備用。
❷ 鍋熱入油1大匙爆香葱段，入排骨炒數下再入①料，以中火煮約15分鐘，再入蘿蔔續煮約10分鐘即可。

450 g. (1 lb.)　pork ribs
300 g. (²/₃ 1b.)　turnips (daikon)
6 sections　green onion
① 2 C.　water
¹/₄ c.　soy sauce
¹/₂ T.　sugar
¹/₈ t.　salt

❶ Cut the ribs into 3 cm (1¹/₃") long strips; blanch in boiling water and then drain. Pare the turnips, then cut them into bite-size pieces.
❷ Heat the wok, then add 1 T. of oil; stir fry the green onion until fragrant. Fry the ribs, then add ① and stir to mix; cook for 15 minutes over medium heat. Add the turnips and cook for another 10 minutes, then serve.

珍肉蘿蔔 (圖右上 illus. right up)
Grounded Pork with Turnips

❶ 白蘿蔔切成0.5公分厚之環狀，入開水煮至透明狀（用筷子可插入），盛起置盤；湯汁留1杯備用。

❷ 鍋熱入油3大匙，入洋葱炒至半熟，隨入絞肉略炒，再入①料及蘿蔔湯汁煮熟，以②料勾芡，起鍋前灑上麻油，再淋於蘿蔔上，撒上香菜葉即可。

❶ Slice the turnips into 0.5 cm ($1/4$") thick round pieces; boil them until soft (chopstick can pierce through); remove and place on a plate. Retain 1 c. of liquid for later use.

❷ Heat the wok, then add 3 T. of oil, stir fry onion. When they are half cooked; stir in the grounded pork and fry for few seconds, then add ① and 1 c. of liquid. Thicken with ② until all the ingredients are cooked. Add sesame oil and pour over the top of turnips. Finally, sprinkle the coriander on the dish. Serve.

白蘿蔔（淨重）···350公克
絞肉················190公克
洋葱丁···········150公克
麻油、香菜葉······各少許

① 醬油·········3大匙
糖···········1/2大匙
鹽···········1/4小匙
胡椒粉········少許

② 水···········1大匙
太白粉········1小匙

350 g. ($2/3$ lb.)	turnips
190 g. ($1/2$ lb.)	grounded pork
150 g. ($1/3$ lb.)	minced onion
a little each	sesame oil, coriander leaves

① 3 T. soy sauce
1/2 T. sugar
1/4 t. salt
Dash pepper

② 1 T. water
1 t. corn starch

栗子燒肉 (圖右下 illus. right down)
Pork with Chestnuts

❶ 五花肉洗淨切塊，入熱水川燙備用。

❷ 鍋熱入油2大匙，爆香葱段、薑片，續入五花肉拌炒數下，再入栗子及①料煮開後，改以小火煮約30分鐘至肉爛即可。

■ 如果用乾栗子，洗淨後放入小碗中，加水滿過栗子入電鍋（外鍋放1碗水）蒸軟，以牙籤將內殼挑淨即可。

❶ Wash the pork, then cut into cubes. Blanch in boiling water and drain.

❷ Heat the wok, then add 2 T. of oil. Stir fry the onion and ginger until fragrant. Add the pork and stir quickly. Mix in the chestnuts and ① then bring them to a boil. Turn the heat to low, cook for 30 minutes, or until the meat is soft. Remove and serve.

■ Dried chestnuts can be used. Wash the dried chestnuts and place them in a bowl. Add water to cover the chestnuts, heat them in a rice cooker (or steamer). Remove when soft and use a tooth pick to peel off the skins.

五花肉·········450公克
罐頭栗子······200公克
葱段···········12段
薑片···········6片

① 水·········3杯
醬油·······3大匙
酒·········1大匙
糖·········1小匙
味精·······1/4小匙

450 g. (1 lb.)	bacon slab
200 g. (7 oz.)	canned chestnut
12 sections	green onion
6 slices	ginger

① 3 c. water
3 T. soy sauce
1 T. cooking wine
1 t. sugar

冬瓜燒肉
Pork With Wintermelon

冬瓜（淨重）……375公克
絞肉………………30公克
蒜末………………1大匙
薑末………………½大匙

① { 太白粉………1小匙
    鹽、味精……各¼小匙
    麻油…………少許

② { 水……………2杯
    酒、醬油……各1大匙

❶ 冬瓜切成2公分塊狀；絞肉以①料醃約10分鐘備用。
❷ 鍋熱入油2大匙，爆香蒜末、薑末，入絞肉炒半熟，續入冬瓜拌炒數下，再入②料，以中火將冬瓜燜至軟透即可。

❶ Peel the wintermelon and then cut into 2 cm (³/₄") cubs. Marinate the grounded pork in ① for 10 minutes.
❷ Heat the wok, then add 2 T. of oil, stir fry garlic and ginger until fragrant. Fry the pork for few seconds, mix in wintermelon and ②. Cook over medium heat until the wintermelom is soft.

375 g. (13¼ oz.) wintermelon
30 g. (1 oz.) grounded pork
1 T. minced garlic
½ T. minced ginger

① { 1 t. corn starch
    ¼ t salt
    Dash sesame oil

② { 2 c. water
    1 T.each cooking wine, soy sauce

6人份 Serves 6

6人份 Serves 6

芝蔴肉片
Sesame Pork Slices

里肌肉………………220公克

① { 蛋白………………1個
    太白粉……………1大匙
    酒…………………½大匙
    鹽…………………¾小匙
    味精、胡椒粉……各¼小匙

② { 白芝蔴……………5大匙
    太白粉……………4大匙

❶ 里肌肉切0.2×3×3公分薄片，調①料醃約半小時；再將里肌肉正反二面沾②料備用。
❷ 鍋熱入油3杯，待熱以中火將肉片炸熟即可。

220 g. (7²/₃ oz.) lean pork

① { 1 egg white
    1 T. corn starch
    ½ T. cooking wine
    ¾ t. salt
    ¼ t. pepper

② { 5 T. white sesame seeds
    4 T. corn starch

❶ Slice lean pork into 0.2x3x3 cm (¹/₁₆"x ¹/₈"x ¹/₈") thin pieces, marinate in ① for 30 minutes. Sprinkle ② over pork slices evenly.
❷ Heat 3 c. of oil in the wok. Deep fry the pork slices over medium heat until cooked.

糖醋荔枝肉
Sweet and Sour Lychee Pork

里肌肉·····················300公克
頭荔枝·····················285公克
白粉·······················6大匙
菜葉·······················少許
{ 蛋黃·····················1個
{ 酒、醬油·················各1大匙

{ 高湯·····················⅔杯
{ 糖、醋、蕃茄醬··········各3大匙
{ 酒、荔枝汁···············各1大匙
{ 鹽·······················1小匙
{ 水·······················3大匙
{ 太白粉···················1大匙

0 g. (⅔ lb.) lean pork
5 g. (10 oz.) canned lychee
T.   corn starch
ittle   coriander leaves
{ 1   egg yolk
{ 1 T. each   cooking wine,
              soy sauce
{ ⅔ c.   stock
{ 3 T. each   sugar, vinegar, ketchup
{ 1 T. each   cooking wine,
              canned lychee juice
{ 1 t.   salt
{ 3 T. water
{ 1 T. corn starch

❶ 里肌肉切成2×2公分大小，入①料醃20分鐘，再沾裹太白粉（圖1）備用；鍋熱入油6杯，待熱，將肉塊炸至表皮呈金黃色且熟透，撈起瀝油備用。
❷ 將②料煮開，入荔枝及肉塊快速攪拌數下，再以③料勾芡，起鍋前撒上香菜葉即可。

❶ Cut the pork into 2 x 2 cm (³/₄" x ³/₄") cubes, marinate in ① for 20 minutes. Roll in the corn starch(illus. 1). Heat 6 c. of oil in the wok. Deep fry the pork until cooked and the color turns to brown; remove and drain.
❷ Add ② to the wok and bring to a boil. Mix in the lychee and pork, then stir quickly. Thicken with ③, then sprinkle on the coriander before serving.

棉花肉
Spongy Pork

里肌肉⋯⋯⋯⋯⋯200公克
蛋白⋯⋯⋯⋯⋯⋯4個
葱絲⋯⋯⋯⋯⋯⋯1杯

① ┌ 酒⋯⋯⋯⋯⋯1大匙
　 │ 鹽⋯⋯⋯⋯⋯½小匙
　 │ 葱段⋯⋯⋯⋯4段
　 └ 薑片⋯⋯⋯⋯3片

② ┌ 高湯⋯⋯⋯⋯¼杯
　 │ 淡色醬油⋯⋯1小匙
　 │ 味精⋯⋯⋯⋯½小匙
　 │ 鹽⋯⋯⋯⋯⋯¼小匙
　 └ 胡椒粉⋯⋯⋯少許

③ ┌ 水⋯⋯⋯⋯⋯2小匙
　 └ 太白粉⋯⋯⋯1小匙

200 g. (7 oz.)	lean pork	
4	egg whites	
1 c.	shredded green onions	
①	1 T.	cooking wine
	½ t.	salt
	4 sections	green onion
	3 slices	ginger
②	¼ c.	stock
	1 t.	light soy sauce
	¼ t.	salt
	Dash	pepper
③	2 t.	water
	1 t.	corn starch

❶ 里肌肉去筋洗淨，加①料拌勻，入蒸籠蒸約30分鐘取出，待涼後撕成細絲狀(圖1) 備用；蛋白拌勻備用。
❷ 鍋熱入油3大匙，入蛋白拌炒數下，再入肉絲及②料拌勻，以③料勾芡，起鍋前撒上葱絲即可。

❶ Remove the white sinews of the lean pork and wash; mix in ① evenly. Steam for 30 minutes; remove. When it is cold tear into shreds(illus. 1). Beat the egg whites lighly.
❷ Heat the wok, then add 3 T. of oil. Stir in the egg white for few seconds then add meat and ②; mix thoroughly. Thicken with ③. Sprinkle on green onion before serving.

❶

五味排骨
Spicy Pork Ribs

小排骨‥‥‥‥‥‥‥‥‥‥400公克
蒜末‥‥‥‥‥‥‥‥‥‥‥‥1大匙

① ┌ 蛋白‥‥‥‥‥‥‥‥‥‥1個
   │ 太白粉‥‥‥‥‥‥‥‥‥2大匙
   │ 酒‥‥‥‥‥‥‥‥‥‥‥1小匙
   └ 鹽‥‥‥‥‥‥‥‥‥‥½小匙

② ┌ 高湯‥‥‥‥‥‥‥‥‥‥2大匙
   │ 糖、酒、醬油、麻油、蕃茄醬、
   │ 辣醬油、芝麻醬‥‥‥各1大匙
   │ 醋‥‥‥‥‥‥‥‥‥‥½大匙
   │ 芥末、咖哩粉‥‥‥‥‥各½小匙
   └ 鹽、胡椒粉‥‥‥‥‥各少許

400 g. (14 oz.) pork ribs
1 T.   minced garlic

① ┌ 1   egg white
   │ 2 T.   corn starch
   │ 1 t.   cooking wine
   └ ½ t. salt

② ┌ 2 T.   stock
   │ 1 T. each sugar, cooking wine,
   │   soy sauce, sesame
   │   oil, ketchup, hot soy
   │   sauce, sesame paste
   │ ½ T.   vinegar
   │ ½ t. each mustard,
   │   curry powder
   └ Dash each salt, pepper

❶ 先將小排骨洗淨瀝乾，入①料拌勻；鍋熱入油4杯，將排骨炸至表皮呈金黃
　 色且熟透，撈起瀝油（圖1），盛盤備用。
❷ 鍋內留油2大匙，爆香蒜末，入②料拌勻，淋於排骨上即可。

❶ Wash the pork ribs, then cut them into 3 cm (1⅓") long strips. Mix thoroughly in ①. Heat 4 c. of oil in the wok, then deep fry the ribs until cooked, and the color turns to brown; remove and drain(illus. 1) Place them on a plate.
❷ Retain 2 T. of oil in the wok, Stir fry the garlic until fragrant, then add ② and mix thoroughly. Pour over the ribs and serve.

金菇炒肉絲

Shredded Pork with Golden Mushrooms

金針菇……………160公克
里肌肉絲…………150公克
筍絲………………50公克
葱絲………………¼杯
麻油、香菜葉……各少許

① {
蛋白…………½個
水……………1大匙
太白粉………½大匙
鹽、味精……各⅛小匙
胡椒粉………少許
}

② {
水……………1大匙
鹽……………½小匙
味精…………¼小匙
胡椒粉………少許
}

160 g. (5½ oz.)
　　Golden mushrooms
150 g. (5¼ oz.)
　　shredded lean pork
50 g. (1¾ oz.)
　　shredded bamboo shoot
¼ c.
　　shredded green onion
a little each
　　sesame oil, coriander leaves

① {
½　　　egg white
1 T.　　water
½ T.　　corn starch
⅛ t.　　salt
Dash　pepper
}

② {
1 T.　　water
½ t.　　salt
Dash　pepper
}

❶ 肉絲以①料醃20分鐘；金針菇切除根部，再切成2段（圖1）洗淨備用。
❷ 鍋熱入油2大匙，續入肉絲炒至肉色變白盛起；用餘油爆香葱絲，入金針菇、筍絲及②料拌勻，再入肉絲拌炒至熟，起鍋前灑上麻油及香菜葉即可。

❶ Marinate the shredded pork in ① for 20 minutes. Cut off the tough root portions from the golden mushrooms; then cut them into 2 sections (illus. 1). Wash and set aside.
❷ Heat the wok, then add 2 T. of oil. Stir fry the pork until the color turns to white; remove. Reheat the remaining oil in the wok. Fry the onions, then add the golden mushrooms, bamboo shoots and ②; mix thoroughly. Stir in the pork and mix quickly. Remove when cooked; sprinkle on the sesame oil and coriander; serve.

洋芋炸丸
Potato Croquettes

6人份 Serves 6

絞肉‧‧‧‧‧‧‧‧‧‧‧‧150公克
馬鈴薯‧‧‧‧‧‧‧‧‧‧150公克
洋葱末‧‧‧‧‧‧‧‧‧‧50公克
紅蘿蔔末、麵粉
　麵包粉‧‧‧‧‧‧‧各30公克
蝦仁‧‧‧‧‧‧‧‧‧‧‧‧25公克
蛋‧‧‧‧‧‧‧‧‧‧‧‧‧‧1個
　鹽、麻油‧‧‧各½小匙
①　味精‧‧‧‧‧‧‧‧¼小匙
　胡椒粉‧‧‧‧‧‧⅛小匙
②　奶粉‧‧‧‧‧‧‧‧1大匙
　太白粉‧‧‧‧‧‧½大匙

150 g. (5⅓ oz.) grounded pork
150 g. (5⅓ oz.) potatoes
50 g. (1⅔ oz.) minced onion
30 g. (1 oz.) each minced carrots,
flour, fine bread
crumbs
25 g. (¾ oz.) shrimps
egg
① { ½ t. each salt, sesame oil
{ ⅛ t. pepper
② { 1 T. milk power
{ ½ T. corn starch

❶ 絞肉剁至有黏性；馬鈴薯去皮切片，煮熟壓成泥；蝦仁切碎；蛋打散備用。
❷ 鍋熱入油1大匙，入絞肉，續入洋葱炒香，再入蝦仁、紅蘿蔔炒熟，入①料調味，盛起瀝乾；入馬鈴薯泥及②料拌勻，做成12個丸子備用。
❸ 將丸子依序沾上麵粉、蛋液（圖1）、麵包粉（圖2）。油4杯燒至8分熱（約160℃，320℉）入芋丸，炸至金黃色即可。

❶ Chop the pork finely until the texture becomes sticky. Pare the potatoes, slice, and steam until soft, then mash. Chop the shrimps finely.
❷ Heat the wok, then add 1 T. of oil, stir fry the pork, then add onion. When fragrance arises, add the shrimps and carrots. Mix in ① when cooked; remove and drain. Blend well with potatoes and ②. Divide into 12 portions, mold each portion into a ball.
❸ Heat the oil to 320°F (160°C). Dip the croquettes first in flour, then the egg (illus. 1), and finally the fine bread crumbs (illus. 2). Deep fry until golden. Remove and serve.

5

里肌紫菜捲
Pork—Nori Rolls

6人份 Serves 6

里肌肉·················120公克
熟紅蘿蔔··············20公克
紫菜·····················2張
熱狗·····················4條
蛋·························1個
蔥白（12公分）······2支
麵糊·····················¼杯

① {
水·····················1大匙
醬油、太白粉···各1小匙
酒、麻油·········各½小匙
鹽·····················¼小匙
胡椒粉···········少許
}

120g. (4¼ oz.) lean pork
20 g. (⅔ oz.)   precooked carrot
2 sheets   purple laver
                seaweed (nori)
4   hot dogs
1   egg
2 stalks (12 cm or 4¾")
                green onion (white section only)
¼ c.   flour paste

① {
1 T.   water
1 t. each   soy sauce
                corn starch
½ t. each   cooking wine,
                sesame oil
¼ t.   salt
Dash   pepper
}

❶ 里肌肉切薄片，加①料醃20分鐘；紅蘿蔔切條狀；蛋打散，煎成2張薄蛋皮備用。
❷ 紫菜攤開，於½處依序鋪上里肌肉、蛋皮、紅蘿蔔、熱狗、蔥白（圖1），再捲成圓筒狀（圖2），接口處以麵糊黏緊；共做2份備用。
❸ 鍋熱入油6杯，入紫菜捲炸熟撈起待涼，切片即可。

❶ Slice the pork into thin pieces and marinate in ① for 20 minutes. Cut the carrot into long strips. Beat the egg until blended. Divide the egg into two portions. Fry separately in a pan to make two crepes.
❷ Place 1 portion of pork, crepe, carrot, hot dog and onion at the center of purple laver seaweed (illus 1). Roll into a long cylinder (illus 2). Seal with the flour paste. Makes two rolls.
❸ Heat 6 c. of oil in the wok and deep fry the rolls. Remove and drain when cooked. Slice the rolls into small pieces when they are cold.

36

生溜里肌
Sliced Pork in Wine Sauce

6人份 Serves 6

里肌肉·················175公克
小黃瓜·················70公克
木耳（乾）···········6朵
或（濕，圖1）······100公克
蒜末·················2小匙

① { 蛋白·················½個
酒、太白粉······各1小匙
鹽·················¼小匙 }

② { 高湯·················¾杯
鹽·················½小匙
糖·················¼小匙
味精·················¹⁄₈小匙 }

③ 水、太白粉各1大匙

175 g. (¹⁄₃ lb.)   lean pork
70 g. (2¹⁄₂ oz.)   gherkin cucumbers
6 pieces   dried wood ears
     [or 100 g. (3¹⁄₂ oz.)
     soft wood ears (illus.1)]
2 t.   minced garlic

① { ¹⁄₂   egg white
1 t. each   cooking wine, corn starch
¹⁄₄ t.   salt }

② { ³⁄₄ c. stock
¹⁄₂ t. salt
¹⁄₄ t. sugar }

③ 1 T. each   water, corn starch

❶

❶ 里肌肉切片，稍拍軟，入①料醃約20分鐘；小黃瓜斜切薄片；木耳泡軟，去蒂，切成肉片大小備用。
❷ 鍋熱入油3大匙，炒熟肉片撈起，餘油入蒜末爆香，再入小黃瓜、木耳、及②料煮沸，入肉片後以③料勾芡即可。

❶ Slice the pork into thin pieces. Then pound slightly Marinate in ① for about 20 minutes. Cut the cucumbers into slanting slices Soak the wood ears in warm water until soft, then cut off the stems. Slice them to the same size as the pork.
❷ Heat the wok, then add 3 T. of oil. Stir fry the meat until cooked; remove the pork. Reheat the remaining oil, fry the garlic until fragrant. Add the cucumbers, wood ears and ②, bring them to a boil. Return the pork to the wok and quickly stir to mix the ingredients. Thicken with ③ and serve.

烤雞腿（圖右上 illus. right up）
Baked Chicken Legs

❶ 雞腿洗淨，內側劃開一刀，入①料醃約半小時備用。
❷ 開烤箱，待溫度上升至190℃（約380℉）後，將醃好的雞腿表面向下，放在烤盤上，烤約15分鐘後再翻面，續烤15分鐘即可。

❶ Score the chicken at the inner side of the legs and thighs. Place the chicken in ① and marinate for about 30 minutes.
❷ Preheat the oven to 380°F (190°C). Place the marinated chicken in a baking dish, outer surface down. Bake 15 minutes in the oven, then remove to turn over the meat. Bake for another 15 minutes. Serve.

大雞腿⋯⋯⋯⋯⋯⋯3隻(850公克)
① 葱段⋯⋯⋯⋯⋯⋯12段
　 薑片⋯⋯⋯⋯⋯⋯3片
　 醬油⋯⋯⋯⋯⋯⋯4大匙
　 蒜末⋯⋯⋯⋯⋯⋯1½大匙
　 酒⋯⋯⋯⋯⋯⋯⋯1大匙
　 糖、花椒粒⋯⋯⋯各½大匙
　 鹽、五香粉⋯⋯⋯各1小匙

3 (850 g. or 1 1b. 14 oz.)
chicken legs with thighs

①		
12 sections	green onion
3 slices	ginger
4 T.	soy sauce
1½ T.	mince garlic
1 T.	cooking wine
½ T. each	sugar, peppercorns
1 t. each	salt, Chinese five-spice powder

黃花沙茶雞 (圖左 illus. left)
Sha Cha Chicken Salad

雞胸肉·················150公克
小黃瓜·················120公克
金針···················25公克

① 沙茶醬·············1½大匙
　醬油、白醋······各1小匙
　味精·············½小匙
　鹽···············¼小匙

❶ 雞胸肉蒸熟，待涼撕成絲；小黃瓜切細絲；金針泡軟去梗切對半，再以開水燙熟備用。
❷ 金針置盤底，上置雞絲，再排上黃瓜絲，食時淋上①料，拌勻即可。

❶ Steam the chicken until cooked, then tear into fine shreds. Slice cucumbers into fine strips. Soak the dried lily buds until soft and trim off the tough ends. Then slice them in half. Blanch in boiling water until cooked.
❷ Place lily buds on a plate. Place the chicken and cucumbers, in order on top of lily buds. Mix ① thoroughly and pour over chicken before eating.

150 g. (⅓ 1b.)   chicken breast fillets
120g.(¼ 1b.)   gherkin cucumbers.
25 g. (¾ oz.)   dried lily buds.

① 1½ T.   Chinese barbecue sauce (sha cha sauce)
1 t. each   soy sauce, white vinegar
¼ t. each   salt, sugar.

核桃雞丁 (圖右下 illus. right down)
Stir—Fried Chicken With Walnuts

雞胸肉·····················300公克
蔥段·······················6段
炸核桃·····················⅔杯
小黃瓜丁···················½杯

① 水、太白粉···········各1大匙
　酒···················½大匙
　鹽···················⅓小匙

② 水···················2大匙
　太白粉···············1小匙
　鹽、糖···············各½小匙
　麻油、味精、胡椒粉······各少許

❶ 雞胸肉拍鬆，切粗丁，入①料拌勻，炒前拌入1大匙油；②料置碗內調勻備用。
❷ 鍋熱入油½杯，入雞丁翻炒至熟，撈出備用；鍋內留油1大匙，爆香蔥段，入小黃瓜丁炒1分鐘，續入雞肉及②料，以大火迅速拌炒，起鍋前加入核桃略拌即可。

❶ Pound the chicken breast fillets to tenderize them, then cut them into ½" cubes. Marinate in ① and mix thoroughly. Before frying, add 1 T. oil. Mix ② in a bowl and set aside for later use.
❷ Heat the wok, then add ½ c. oil. Stir fry the chicken until cooked; then remove. Retain 1 T. of oil in the wok. Stir fry onion until fragrant. Add cucumbers and stir fry for about 1 minute. Add chicken and ② Turn heat to high, and quickly sitr fry. Add fried walnuts and mix. Remove and serve.

300 g. (⅔ 1b.)   chicken breast fillets
6 sections   green onion
⅔ c.   fried walnuts
½ c.   cubed gherkin cucumbers

① 1 T. each   water, corn starch
½ T.   cooking wine
⅓ t.   salt

② 2 T.   water
1 t.   corn starch
½ t. each   salt, sugar
Dash each   sesame oil, pepper

芷薑鴨塊（圖左 illus. left）
Ginger Braised Duckling

鴨	……………半隻（約750公克）
薑片	……………150公克
麻油	……………4大匙

①
- 水……………3杯
- 酒……………2大匙
- 糖、醬油……各1大匙
- 鹽、味精……各½小匙

❶ 鴨切塊，入開水川燙，撈起備用。
❷ 麻油燒熱，爆香薑片，入鴨塊略炒，續入①料，大火煮開，再改小火燜約1小時，至鴨肉爛即可。

½ (750 g. or 1²⁄₃ lb.)	duckling
150 g. (⅓ lb.)	sliced ginger
4 T.	sesame oil

①
3 c.	water
2 T.	cooking wine
1 T. each	sugar, soy sauce
½ t.	salt

❶ Chop the duckling into pieces. Blanch them in boiling water; remove and drain.
❷ Heat the sesame oil, stir fry the ginger until fragrant. Fry the duckling briefly then add ①. Bring to a boil then turn the heat to low; cook for an hour, or until it is tender.

枇杷雞腿 (圖右上 illus. right up)
Loquat Chicken

❶ 雞小腿由內面將肉剝離骨，肉往上推使雞骨露出，續打鬆腿肉，再以①料醃10分鐘備用。
❷ 將雞肉依太白粉、蛋液、麵包粉的順序沾裹均勻。油3杯燒至7分熱(約140℃，280℉)，入雞肉，以中火炸至表皮呈金黃色，撈起置盤中，以蝦餅圍邊即可。

❶ Score the chicken at the end of drum sticks, then push the meat up to form a loquat shape. Pound the drum sticks to tenderize them, then marinate in ① for 10 minutes.
❷ Roll the marinated drum sticks first in the corn starch then in the egg, finally in fine bread crumbs. Heat the oil in the wok up to 280°F (140°C). Deep fry the drum sticks until cooked and the color is golden brown; remove and drain. Arrange on a serving plate with shrimp chips.

雞小腿	⋯⋯⋯⋯⋯	6隻
蝦餅	⋯⋯⋯⋯⋯	6片
太白粉、麵包粉	⋯⋯⋯	各3大匙
蛋(打勻)	⋯⋯⋯⋯	1個

①
- 葱段⋯⋯⋯⋯⋯⋯6段
- 薑片⋯⋯⋯⋯⋯⋯2片
- 酒⋯⋯⋯⋯⋯⋯⋯1大匙
- 鹽、味精⋯⋯⋯各1小匙

6	chicken drum sticks
6	fried shrimp chips
3 T. each	corn starch, fine bread crumbs
1	egg (lightly beaten)

①
- 6 sections green onion
- 2 slices ginger
- 1 T. cooking wine
- 1 t. salt

香酥雞翅 (圖右下 illus. right down)
Crispy Chicken Wing

❶ 雞翅洗淨，拭乾水分，抹上醬油備用。
❷ 鍋熱入油4杯，燒至7分熱(約140℃，280℉)，入雞翅炸約10分鐘至表皮呈金黃色，撈起置盤，淋上①料即可。

■ 喜好辣味者，可加1小匙辣油入①料。

❶ Rinse, clean and drain the chicken wings, then rub soy sauce on the wings.
❷ Heat 4 C. of oil in the wok until it is 280°F (140°C). Fry the wings until golden brown, then drain and place on platter. Pour ① on top of the chicken.

■ Add 1 t. hot pepper sauce in ①, if you prefer a hot flavor.

雞翅	⋯⋯⋯⋯12隻	(約600公克)
醬油	⋯⋯⋯⋯½大匙	

①
- 葱末 ⋯⋯¼杯
- 醬油 ⋯⋯2½大匙
- 醋 ⋯⋯⋯2大匙
- 糖 ⋯⋯⋯1½大匙
- 薑末 ⋯⋯1大匙
- 麻油 ⋯⋯1小匙

12 (600g. or 1⅓ 1b.)		chicken wings
½ T.		soy sauce

①
- ¼ c. minced green onion
- 2½ T. soy sauce
- 2 T. vinegar
- 1½ T. sugar
- 1 T. minced ginger
- 1 t. sesame oil

桂花雞絲
Chicken Foo Yung

雞胸肉（去皮）⋯⋯⋯⋯⋯⋯120公克
蛋⋯⋯⋯⋯⋯⋯⋯⋯⋯⋯⋯⋯⋯2個
香菜葉（圖1）⋯⋯⋯⋯⋯⋯2大匙

① 香菇（泡軟切絲）⋯⋯⋯⋯4朵
　 筍絲、洋葱絲⋯⋯⋯⋯⋯各40公克
　 葱絲、火腿絲⋯⋯⋯⋯⋯各20公克

② 水⋯⋯⋯⋯⋯⋯⋯⋯⋯⋯⋯1小匙
　 酒、醬油、太白粉⋯⋯⋯各½小匙
　 鹽、糖⋯⋯⋯⋯⋯⋯⋯各1／8小匙
　 胡椒粉⋯⋯⋯⋯⋯⋯⋯⋯少許

③ 醬油⋯⋯⋯⋯⋯⋯⋯⋯⋯½大匙
　 鹽、糖⋯⋯⋯⋯⋯⋯⋯各¼小匙

120 g. (¹/₄ lb.) chicken breast fillets
2   eggs
2 T.   coriander leaves

① ³/₄ oz.
      shredded mushrooms (soak
      the dry mushrooms until soft
      then shred)
   40 g. (1¹/₂ oz.) each
      shredded bamboo shoot,
      shredded onion
   20 g. (³/₄ oz.) each
      shredded green onion,
      shredded ham

② 1 t.   water
   ¹/₂ t. each   cooking wine, soy
                    sauce, corn starch
   ¹/₈ t. each   salt, sugar
   Dash   pepper

③ ¹/₂ T.   soy sauce
   ¹/₄ t. each   salt, sugar

❶ 雞胸肉切細絲，加②料醃15分鐘；蛋打散備用。
❷ 鍋熱入油½杯，燒至7分熱（約140℃，280℉），入雞絲泡熟撈起；鍋內留油3大匙，入蛋液炒熟，續入①料拌炒2分鐘，再加雞絲及③料拌勻，起鍋前撒上香菜葉即可。

❶ Shred the chicken and then marinate in ② for 15 minutes. Beat the eggs lightly.
❷ Heat the wok, then add ¹/₂ c. of oil, heat the oil up to 280°F (140°C). Add the chicken and when cooked, remove it and drain. Retain 3 T. of oil in the wok, stir fry the beaten egg then add ①, fry for 2 minutes. Add chicken and ③, mix thoroughly, sprinkle on the coriander remove and serve.

葡國雞片
Coconut Chicken Fritters　6人份 Serves 6

雞胸肉⋯⋯⋯⋯⋯⋯⋯⋯150公克
太白粉⋯⋯⋯⋯⋯⋯⋯⋯½杯
蛋黃(打散)⋯⋯⋯⋯⋯⋯2個

① 葱薑汁⋯⋯⋯⋯⋯⋯3大匙
　 鹽、糖⋯⋯⋯⋯⋯各½小匙
　 麻油、胡椒粉⋯⋯⋯各少許

② 椰子粉⋯⋯⋯⋯⋯⋯1杯
　 白葡萄乾(先泡水瀝乾)
　 、核桃末⋯⋯⋯⋯各½杯

③ 水⋯⋯⋯⋯⋯⋯⋯⋯¾杯
　 糖⋯⋯⋯⋯⋯⋯⋯⋯3大匙
　 檸檬汁⋯⋯⋯⋯⋯⋯1大匙

④ 水⋯⋯⋯⋯⋯⋯⋯⋯2小匙
　 太白粉⋯⋯⋯⋯⋯⋯1小匙

150 g. (⅓ 1b.)　chicken breast fillets
½ c.　　　　　corn starch
2　　　　　　egg yolks
① 3 T.　　　onion with ginger juice
　 ½ t. each　salt, sugar
　 Dash each　sesame oil, pepper
② 1 c.　　　desiccated (or flaked) coconut
　 ½ c. each　white raisins, minced walnuts
③ ¾ c.　water
　 3 T.　sugar
　 1 T.　lemon juice
④ 2 t.　water
　 1 t.　corn starch

❶ 雞胸肉洗淨切薄片，加①料醃10分鐘；再依序沾上太白粉、蛋黃及②料備用。油4杯燒至7分熱(140℃，280℉)，入雞片，炸至金黃色，撈起置盤。將③料煮開，以④料勾芡，淋於雞片上即可。

■葱薑汁處理法：

葱⋯⋯⋯8段
薑片⋯⋯3片
水⋯⋯⋯3大匙

❶ 葱洗淨略拍；薑片亦略拍；一起泡入水中(圖1)至出味，再撈出葱段及薑片，湯汁留用即為葱薑汁。

❶ Rinse the chicken and slice into thin pieces. Then marinate in ① for 10 minutes. Dip the marinated chicken first into corn starch, then egg yolks, and finally in the mixture ②.

❷ Heat 4 c. of oil in the wok to 280°F (140°C). Deep fry the chicken until golden brown. Remove and place on a plate. Bring ③ to a boil and mix in ④ to thicken. Pour it on top of the chicken.

Onion with Ginger Juice

8 sections　green onion
3 slices　　ginger
3 T.　　　water

❶ Crush the onion and ginger and add to the water (illus.1). Soak until a fragrance arises. Then remove onion and ginger.

翡翠雞
Jaded Chicken

雞‥‥‥‥‥‥‥‥1斤
葱段‥‥‥‥‥‥110公克
薑片‥‥‥‥‥‥10公克
麻油‥‥‥‥‥‥少許

① ｛ 水‥‥‥‥‥1杯
　　 酒‥‥‥‥‥¾杯
　　 白醋‥‥‥‥1小匙

② ｛ 醬油露‥‥‥2小匙
　　 糖‥‥‥‥‥1小匙
　　 鹽‥‥‥‥‥½小匙
　　 味精‥‥‥‥⅛小匙

③ ｛ 水‥‥‥‥‥1大匙
　　 太白粉‥‥‥1小匙

600 g. (1⅓ 1b.) chicken
110 g. (4 oz.)　green onion
10 g. (⅓ oz.)　sliced ginger
Dash　　　　 sesame oil

① ｛ 1 c.　water
　　 ¾ c.　cooking wine
　　 1 t.　vinegar

② ｛ 2 t.　soy sauce
　　 1 t.　sugar
　　 ½ t.　salt

③ ｛ 1 T.　water
　　 1 t.　corn starch

❶ 雞洗淨剁塊(圖1)備用。

❷ 鍋熱入油3大匙，爆香薑片，入雞塊炒至半熟，續入①料，改小火燜煮15分鐘；待雞塊熟後，入②料調味，再入葱段拌炒數下，以③料勾芡，起鍋前淋上麻油即可。

❶ Rinse Chicken and chop it into pieces(illus. 1).

❷ Heat the wok, then add 3 T. of oil. Stir fry ginger until fragrant then add chicken. Fry chicken for few minutes; add ① and bring to a boil, cover and turn heat to low. Cook for 15 minutes. When cooked, stir mix with ② and green onion. Thicken with ③, sprinkle sesame oil over the top and serve.

❶

雞絨扒鮮奶
Chicken Over Steamed Egg

雞胸肉(去皮)‥‥‥‥‥‥100公克
香菇‥‥‥‥‥‥‥‥‥‥‥5公克
鮮奶‥‥‥‥‥‥‥‥‥‥‥1½杯
蛋白‥‥‥‥‥‥‥‥‥‥‥3個

①{ 水‥‥‥‥‥‥‥‥‥‥1大匙
　 鹽、酒、太白粉‥‥‥各½小匙
　 味精‥‥‥‥‥‥‥‥‥¹/₈小匙

②{ 水‥‥‥‥‥‥‥‥‥‥½杯
　 麻油‥‥‥‥‥‥‥‥‥½小匙
　 鹽‥‥‥‥‥‥‥‥‥‥¼小匙
　 味精‥‥‥‥‥‥‥‥‥1/₈小匙
　 胡椒粉‥‥‥‥‥‥‥‥少許

③{ 水‥‥‥‥‥‥‥‥‥‥¼杯
　 太白粉‥‥‥‥‥‥‥‥1小匙

100 g. (3½ oz.)
　 chicken breast fillets
5 g. (¼ oz.)
　 dried black mushrooms
1½ c.　fresh milk
3　　　egg whites

①{ 1 T.　　　　water
　 ½ t. each　salt, cooking wine,
　　　　　　　corn starch

②{ ½ c.　water
　 ½ t.　sesame oil
　 ¼ t.　salt
　 Dash　pepper

③{ ¼ c.　water
　 1 t.　corn starch

❶ 雞胸肉洗淨剁成絨狀(圖1)，以①料醃約10分鐘；香菇泡軟切小丁備用。
❷ 蛋白及奶水輕輕攪拌均勻，倒入深盤中，入蒸籠，以小火蒸約15分鐘，取出備用。
❸ 鍋熱入油2大匙，爆香香菇撈起後，關火；待油鍋稍涼，入雞絨及②料拌勻，再開火，並入香菇一起煮開，以③料勾芡，淋於2項材料上即可。

❶ Rinse the chicken clean, chop and pound to a paste (illus. 1), then marinate in ① for about 10 minutes. Soak the dried black mushrooms until soft, remove the stem and cut into small cubes.
❷ Mix the egg white and the fresh milk lightly, pour into a bowl and steam for about 15 minutes over high heat, then remove.
❸ Heat the wok, then add 2 T. of oil, stir fry the mushrooms until fragrant. Turn the heat off, add chicken and ②. Turn the heat on again, add mushrooms, then bring to a boil. Add ③ to thicken, then pour over and serve.

香蒜雞捲
Chicken With Nori Rolls 6人份 Serves 6

雞胸肉	150公克
蒜苗	20公克
紫菜	1張
麵包粉	½杯
太白粉	1大匙
蛋(打散)	1個
① { 鹽	¼小匙
味精、胡椒粉	各⅛小匙

150 g. (⅓ 1b.)	chicken breast fillets
20 g. (⅔ oz.)	garlic leeks
1 sheet	purple laver seaweed (Nori)
½ c.	fine bread crumbs
1 T.	corn starch
1	egg (slightly beaten)
① { ¼ t.	salt
⅛ t.	pepper

❶ 雞胸肉切成兩片(圖1),略拍薄,加①料略醃;蒜苗洗淨斜切弄鬆散(圖2),分成2等份;紫菜對切成兩張備用。

❷ 雞胸肉攤平,上置1份蒜苗及紫菜捲好,依序沾上太白粉、蛋液及麵包粉;共做2份備用。

❸ 鍋熱入油6杯,燒至6分熱(約120℃,240°F),入雞捲以中火炸至金黃色,撈起瀝油,切段排盤即可。

❶ Rinse the chicken clean, slice it into two pieces (illus. 1); pound them to thin pieces. Marinate in ① for few minutes. Wash the leeks, cut into slanting slices, then loosen the leaves (illus. 2); divide into two portions. Cut the purple laver seaweed into pieces.

❷ Spread out the chicken fillets. Roll up one portion of leek and a piece of purple laver seaweed inside each chicken fillet. Roll in the corn starch first, then egg and finally in fine bread crumbs.

❸ Heat 6 c. of oil in the wok up to 240°F (115℃). Deep fry chicken with nori rolls over medium heat; until the color turns to golden brown. Remove and drain, then cut each roll into pieces, arrange on a serving plate.

葱扒鴨塊
Green Onion Braised Duckling

鴨·····················¼隻(約600公克)
醬油、紅辣椒絲·········各2大匙

① ┌ 肉絲·····················50公克
   │ 冬菜(圖1)···········20公克
   │ 葱絲·····················1杯
   └ 薑絲·····················¼杯

② ┌ 醬油·····················2大匙
   │ 酒·······················1大匙
   │ 糖·······················1小匙
   └ 胡椒粉··················少許

③ ┌ 水·······················2大匙
   └ 太白粉··················1小匙

(600 g. or 1⅓1b.) duckling
T. each soy sauce, shredded
        red hot peppers

50 g. (1⅔ oz.)	shredded pork
20 g. (⅔ oz. illus. 1)	preserved vegetable
1 c.	shredded green onion
¼ c.	shredded ginger

2 T.	soy sauce
1 T.	cooking wine
1 t.	sugar
Dash	pepper

| 2 T. | water |
| 1 t. | corn starch |

❶ 鴨洗淨,先入水中煮熟,取出待涼,以醬油塗抹鴨身。五杯油燒至8分熱(160℃,320°F),鴨入油鍋,炸至金黃色,取出剁塊,排入大碗中(圖2)備用。
❷ 鍋內留油3大匙,入①料及紅辣椒絲炒香,續入②料拌勻,再倒於鴨塊上,入蒸籠蒸約2小時取出,倒出湯汁留用,鴨肉倒扣於盤中備用。
❸ 湯汁煮開,以③料勾芡,淋於鴨肉上即可。

❶ Rinse the duckling then boil it until cooked; remove. When it is cold, rub exterior and cavity with soy sauce. Heat 5 c. of oil in the wok up to 320°F (160℃), then deep fry the duckling until golden brown; remove and chop to pieces; arrange it in a bowl (illus. 2).
❷ Retain 3 T. of oil and heat it in the wok; stir fry ① and red hot peppers until fragrant then mix in ② briefly; pour over the duckling. Steam it for 2 hours; remove and retain the broth. Invert on a serving plate.
❸ Bring the broth to a boil, thicken with ③. Pour over the duckling and serve.

香煎雞脯
Sliced Chicken With Vegetable

雞胸肉（去皮）⋯⋯⋯⋯220公克
洋蔥塊⋯⋯⋯⋯⋯⋯⋯120公克
豌豆莢⋯⋯⋯⋯⋯⋯⋯30公克

① {
蛋白⋯⋯⋯⋯⋯⋯½個
太白粉⋯⋯⋯⋯⋯1½大匙
酒⋯⋯⋯⋯⋯⋯⅔大匙
味精、鹽⋯⋯⋯各¼小匙
胡椒粉⋯⋯⋯⋯少許
}

② {
水⋯⋯⋯⋯⋯⋯5大匙
蕃茄醬⋯⋯⋯⋯2大匙
糖⋯⋯⋯⋯⋯1½小匙
黑醋、味精、酒⋯⋯各½小匙
麻油、鹽⋯⋯⋯各⅛小匙
}

220 g. (8 oz.) chicken breast fillets
120 g. (¼ 1b.) cubed onion
30 g (1 oz.)   snow peas

① {
½   egg white
1½ T. corn starch
⅔ T.   cooking wine
¼ t.   salt
Dash   pepper
}

② {
5 T.   water
2 T.   tomato ketchup
1½ t.   sugar
½ t. each   black vinegar,
             cooing wine
⅛ t. each   sesame oil, salt
}

❶ 雞胸肉洗淨切薄片（圖1），入①料醃約半小時；豌豆莢去頭尾，燙熟備用。
❷ 鍋熱入油3大匙，入雞胸肉炒熟盛起，餘油再熱，炒軟洋蔥塊，入②料煮沸再入雞肉片及豌豆莢拌勻即可。

❶ Rinse chicken and slice them into thin pieces(illus.1). Then marinate in ① for 30 minutes. Remove the stems and the strings from the snow peas. Blanch them in boiling water and drain.
❷ Heat the wok and add 3 T. of oil, stir fry the chicken until cooked; remove and drain. Reheat the remains of oil in the wok, fry onion until soft, then add ② and bring to a boil. Stir in chicken and snow peas, mixed well and then serve.

玉米醬燴雞排
Cream of Corn Over Chicken Fillets

雞胸肉···················225公克
蛋·····················1個
太白粉···················¼杯

①
- 葱段···············4段
- 薑片···············2片
- 水················1大匙
- 酒···············1½小匙
- 鹽、糖、味精······各¼小匙
- 胡椒粉············少許

②
- 蛋黃··············1個
- 玉米醬············½杯
- 奶水·············¼杯

225 g. (8 oz.)	chicken breast fillets
1	egg
¼ c.	corn starch

①
4 sections	green onion
2 slices	ginger
1 T.	water
1½ t.	cooking wine
¼ t. each	salt, sugar
Dash	pepper

②
1	egg yolk
½ c.	cream of corn
¼ c.	milk

❶ 蛋打散備用；雞胸肉以搥肉器搥鬆（圖1），加①料醃約20分鐘，再依序沾上蛋液、太白粉。

❷ 鍋熱入油4杯，燒至7分熱（約140℃，280℉），入雞排炸至金黃色，撈起切段排盤，②料拌勻再以小火煮開，淋於雞排上即可。

❶ Beat the egg lightly and set aside. Pound the chicken fillets (illus. 1) to tenderize them, then marinate in ① for 20 minutes. Dip marinated chicken first into the beaten egg, then into the corn starch.

❷ Heat 4 c. of oil in the wok until it is 280°F (140°C). Deep fry chicken until golden brown, then drain and cut into pieces, place on a plate. Mix ② thoroughly, boil it with a low heat, pour over on the chicken fillets and serve.

❶

6人份 Serves 6

京葱粉絲 (圖左 illus. left)
Beef with Bean Thread

牛肉……………150公克
粉絲……………30公克
葱白絲…………1杯
① 水…………¼杯
　 酒、醬油……各2大匙
　 糖…………1大匙

❶ 牛肉切薄片；粉絲泡軟切段備用。
❷ 鍋熱入油3大匙，續入葱白絲炒香，隨入牛肉片及①料拌炒後，加入粉絲
　拌勻至熟即可。

150 g. (⅓ 1b.)   flank steak
30 g. (1 oz.)   bean thread
1 c.   green onions
① ¼ c.   water
   2 T. each cooking wine, soy sauce
   1 T.   sugar

❶ Slice the beef. Soak the bean thread in warm water to soften, then cut it in half. Shred the green onions.
❷ Heat the wok, then add 3 T. of oil. Stir fry onions until fragrant. Add the beef and ①; stir quickly. Mix in the bean thread, remove to a serving plate when cooked.

中式牛柳 (圖右上 illus. right up)
Fillet Beef Cantonese Style

❶ 牛肉洗淨切約1公分條狀，入①料拌勻，醃約半小時；鍋熱入油1杯，隨入牛柳拌炒至半熟撈起瀝油備用。

❷ 鍋內留油2大匙，入洋葱絲炒熟，續入②料煮開，再入牛柳拌勻即可。

❶ Wash the beef then cut into long strips, marinate in ① for 30 minutes. Heat the wok and add 1 c. of oil. Fry the beef until it is done medium beef ; remove and drain.

❷ Heat the wok, then add 2 T. of oil. Stir fry the onions until cooked. Add ② and bring to a boil; mix in the beef and stir quickly. Remove and serve.

牛里肌肉·········300公克
洋葱絲·········¾杯

① { 醬油、水···各1大匙
    酒、太白粉各½大匙

② { 水·····················2大匙
    醬油·················1¼大匙
    蕃茄醬、紅辣椒絲······各1大匙
    糖、醋·················各½大匙

300 g. (²/₃ 1b.) beef tenderloin
¾ c.   shredded onions

① { 1 T. each soy sauce, water
    ½ T. each cooking wine, corn
             starch

② { 2 T.   water
    1¼ T.   soy sauce
    1 T. each ketchup, hot red
               pepper
    ½ T. each sugar, vinegar

京醬牛肉絲 (圖右下 illus. right down)
Shredded Beef with Peking Sauce

❶ 京葱絲泡水，瀝乾水分，舖於盤內；牛肉切絲，入①料醃約10分鐘備用。

❷ 鍋熱入油1杯，以溫油將牛肉絲泡熟撈起，鍋內留油1大匙，將②料煮開，入牛肉絲炒勻，再盛於京葱絲上，食時拌勻即可。

❶ Soak the onions in the water for about 5 minutes; remove. Place the onions on a plate. Shred the beef and mix in ① for about 10 minutes.

❷ Heat the wok, then add 1 c. of oil. Fry the beef over medium heat until done medium well; remove and drain. Retain 1 T. of oil in the wok add ② and bring it to a boil. Mix in the beef thoroughly and pour over the onions. Before serving, mix the onions with the beef.

牛肉·············300克
京葱絲·········1杯

① { 水···········3大匙
    太白粉······1½大匙
    醬油·········1大匙
    酒···········2小匙

② { 甜麵醬······1½大匙
    醬油·········1大匙
    酒···········½大匙
    糖···········2小匙
    味精·········¼小匙

300 g. (²/₃ 1b.) flank steak
1 c.   shredded green
                 onions (white
                 sections only)

① { 3 T.   water
    1½ T.   corn starch
    1 T.   soy sauce
    2 t.   cooking wine

② { 1½ T.   sweet bean paste
    1 T.   soy sauce
    ½ T.   cooking wine
    2 t.   sugar

金芋牛腩（圖左 illus. left）
Beef Stew with Potato

牛腩、馬鈴薯⋯⋯⋯⋯⋯各300公克
水⋯⋯⋯⋯⋯⋯⋯⋯⋯10杯
① { 蒜末、醬油、蕃茄醬‥各2大匙
糖⋯⋯⋯⋯⋯⋯⋯⋯⋯1小匙
胡椒粉⋯⋯⋯⋯⋯⋯⋯¼小匙
② 水、太白粉 ⋯⋯⋯⋯⋯各1大匙

300 g. (²/₃ 1b.) each   stew beef,
                         potatoes
10 c.   water
① { 2 T.   minced garlic, soy sauce,
              ketchup
     1 t.   sugar
     ¹/₄ t.   pepper
②   1 T. each   water, corn starch

❶ 牛腩洗淨，切3公分立方塊；馬鈴薯去皮，切2公分立方塊備用。
❷ 鍋熱入油4杯，燒至150℃（約♭0°F），入馬鈴薯炸熟撈出；再將油燒至
高溫，入馬鈴薯炸至表面呈金黃色，撈起瀝油，置於盤上備用。
❸ 牛腩加水煮約2小時至軟，入①料續煮15分鐘使之入味，再以②料勾芡
淋於馬鈴薯上即可。

❶ Wash the beef and cut into 3 cm (1¹/₃") cubes. Pare the potatoes
cut into 2 cm (³/₄") cubes.
❷ Heat 4 c. of oil in the wok to 300°F (150℃), deep fry the potatoes
until cooked; remove. Fry the potatoes over high heat again until
golden brown; remove and drain. Arrange on a serving platter.
❸ Boil the beef. As soon as the water boils reduce the heat and
simmer for 2 hours, or until tender. Add ① and simmer for another
15 minutes. Thicken with ②. Pour over the potatoes and serve.

蘆筍牛肉 (圖右上 illus. right up)
Beef with Asparagus

❶ 蘆筍去筋切斜片，牛肉切片入①料醃約10分鐘，炒前加1大匙油拌勻。
❷ 鍋熱入油3大匙，先將牛肉炒至七分熟撈起；餘油再熱入蒜片爆香，續入
蘆筍及②料拌炒數下，最後入牛肉炒熟即可。

❶ Cut off the tough portion of asparagus and slice them into pieces at
an slanting angle. Slice the beef and marinate in ① for 10 minutes.
Add 1 T. of oil and mix with the beef, so that it will separate
easily during frying.
❷ Heat the wok, then add 3 T. of oil. Stir fry the beef until done
medium well; remove. Reheat the remainning oil in the wok, fry the
garlic until fragrant. Add asparagus and ②, mix quickly then add beef.
Fry until done and serve.

牛肉‥‥‥‥‥‥‥‥‥175公克
蘆筍‥‥‥‥‥‥‥‥‥150公克
蒜片‥‥‥‥‥‥‥‥‥1大匙
① ｛水‥‥‥‥‥‥‥‥2大匙
醬油‥‥‥‥‥‥‥1大匙
酒、太白粉‥‥‥‥各½大匙
② ｛鹽‥‥‥‥‥‥‥‥½小匙
糖‥‥‥‥‥‥‥‥¼小匙
味精‥‥‥‥‥‥‥⅛小匙

175 g. flank steak
150 g. asparagus
1 T. sliced garlic
① ｛ 2 T. water
1 T. soy sauce
½ T. each cooking wine,
corn starch
② ｛ ½ t. salt
¼ t. sugar

家常牛肉 (圖右下 illus. right down)
Beef With Celery

■ 材料中除了將150公克蘆筍改爲200公克西洋芹菜及6大匙蒜片改爲6片
薑片外，其餘均與蘆筍牛肉相同。
■ 作法也與蘆筍牛肉同。

Ingredients and preparation steps are the same as for "Beef with
Asparagus" except substitute 200 g. celery for 150 g. asparagus, 6
slices ginger for 1 T. sliced garlic.

蠔油芥蘭牛肉
Beef With Broccoli in Oyster Sau

芥蘭·················250公克
牛肉·················175公克
葱段·················6段
薑片·················6片
酒·················½大匙

①
水·············3大匙
醬油·········1大匙
太白粉·········2小匙
酒·············1小匙
小蘇打·········¼小匙

②
蠔油·········1½大匙
水·············1½小匙
太白粉·········1小匙
糖、味精、麻油、
胡椒粉·········各¼小匙

❶ 牛肉洗淨切薄片，入①料醃約1小時，下鍋前加油1大匙拌勻；芥蘭除纖維切長段備用。
❷ 鍋熱入油2杯，入牛肉以中火泡約20秒鐘，至牛肉八分熟時撈出，鍋內留油2大匙，將葱、薑及芥蘭略炒，隨入牛肉、酒及②料炒勻即可。

❶ Wash the beef and slice into thin pieces. Marinate in ① for 1 hour. Then add 1 T. of oil and mix with the beef, so that it will separate easily during frying. Cut off the tough portion of the broccoli, then cut into long pieces.
❷ Heat the wok, then add 2 c. of oil, fry beef over medium heat until medium well; remove. Retain 2 T. of oil in the wok, stir fry the onions, ginger and broccoli quickly. Mix in the beef, cooking wine, and ② thoroughly; and serve.

6人份 Serves 6

250 g. (9 oz.)		broccoli
175 g. (6¼ oz.)		flank steak
6 sections		green onion
6 slices		ginger
½ T.		cooking wine
①	3 T.	water
	1 T.	soy sauce
	2 t.	corn starch
	1 t.	cooking wine
	¼ T.	baking soda
②	1½ T.	oyster sauce
	1½ t.	water
	1 T.	corn starch
	¼ T. each	sugar, sesame oil, pepper

6人份 Serves 6

沙茶牛肉
Beef in Sha Cha Sauce

■ 材料中除了將芥蘭改爲洋葱塊及②料之蠔油改爲沙茶醬外，其餘均與蠔油芥蘭牛肉同。
■ 作法也與蠔油芥蘭牛肉同。

Ingredients and preparation steps are the same as for "Beef with Broccoli in Oyster Sauce", except substitute 1½ T. oyster sauce for the sha cha sauce.

咖哩牛肉盒
Curry Beef in Shell

絞牛肉、洋葱末……各100公克
土司（未切片）……⅓條
水………………3大匙

① { 咖哩粉…………1小匙
　　糖………………½小匙
　　鹽……………³/₈小匙

② { 水………………1小匙
　　太白粉………½小匙

③ { 麵粉…………2大匙
　　水…………1大匙

100 g. (3½ oz.) each　grounded
　　　　　　　　　beef, minced
　　　　　　　　　onion
⅓ loaf　　　　　unsliced toast
3 T.　　　　　　water

① { 1 t.　curry powder
　　½ t.　sugar
　　³/₈ t.　salt

② { 1 t.　water
　　½ t.　corn starch

③ { 2 T.　flour
　　1 T.　water

❶ 鍋熱入油2大匙，炒香洋葱，續入牛肉炒熟，再入①料及水拌勻，以②料勾芡，待冷即為餡；③料調勻成麵糊備用。
❷ 土司冷凍後切0.5公分薄片12片；每片攤開，入蒸籠大火蒸2分鐘取出；每片土司各置1份餡，對折成三角形，接口處以麵糊黏緊（圖1），再以模型壓成半圓形（圖2），入7分熱（約140°C，280°F）油鍋，炸至金黃色即可。

■ 食時可沾蕃茄醬。

❶ Heat the wok, then add 2 T. of oil. Stir fry the onion till fragrant, add in the beef; fry till done. Pour in water and ①, mix it thoroughly and thicken it with ②. When cold, this will be the filling. Work ③ into a thick paste to use.
❷ Freeze the toast and cut into 12 thin slices of 0.5 cm (¼") thick. Spread out the slices in a steamer; steam it over high heat for 2 minutes and remove. Place a filling onto each slice; fold them crosswise into triangles. Seal the openings tightly with the paste (illus. 1), press them into crescent shapes with a mold (illus. 2). Heat the oil to 284°F (140°C), and fry them unit golden brown.

■ May be served with ketchup.

豉椒燴牛肉
Spicy Beef with Black Soybeans

牛肉‥‥‥‥‥‥‥‥‥‥‥180公克
靑椒‥‥‥‥‥‥‥‥‥‥‥75公克
蛋‥‥‥‥‥‥‥‥‥‥‥‥2個
紅辣椒丁‥‥‥‥‥‥‥‥‥½大匙
① { 蒜片、葱末‥‥‥‥‥‥各1½大匙
    豆豉(圖1)、薑末 ‥‥‥各1大匙
② { 水‥‥‥‥‥‥‥‥‥‥2大匙
    醬油‥‥‥‥‥‥‥‥‥1大匙
    小蘇打‥‥‥‥‥‥‥‥½小匙
    鹽‥‥‥‥‥‥‥‥‥‥⅓小匙
    胡椒粉‥‥‥‥‥‥‥‥少許
③ { 水‥‥‥‥‥‥‥‥‥‥1杯
    酒、醬油‥‥‥‥‥‥‥各1大匙
    麻油‥‥‥‥‥‥‥‥‥2小匙
    糖、味精‥‥‥‥‥‥‥各1小匙
    鹽‥‥‥‥‥‥‥‥‥‥½小匙
    胡椒粉‥‥‥‥‥‥‥‥少許
④ { 水‥‥‥‥‥‥‥‥‥‥2大匙
    太白粉‥‥‥‥‥‥‥‥1大匙

180 g. (6⅓ oz.)	beef flank
75 g. (2⅔ oz.)	green pepper
2	eggs
½ T.	diced hot red pepper

①
| 1½ T. each | sliced garlic, minced green onion |
| 1 T. each | black soybean (illus.1), minced ginger |

②
2 T.	water
1 T.	soy sauce
½ t.	baking soda
⅓ t.	salt
Dash	pepper

③
1 C.	water
1 T. each	cooking wine, soy sauce
2 t.	sesame oil
1 t.	sugar
½ t.	salt
Dash	pepper

④
| 2 T. | water |
| 1 T. | corn starch |

❶ 牛肉切薄片，加②料醃半小時；靑椒洗淨去籽切塊；蛋打散備用。
❷ 鍋熱入油2大匙，入靑椒、紅辣椒炒熟，撈起備用；再熱鍋入油3大匙將牛肉炒半熟撈起備用。
❸ 鍋熱入油1大匙，炒香①料，續入③料煮開，再入牛肉拌炒數下後熄火，入蛋液輕輕拌勻，並以④料勾芡，再入靑、紅椒拌勻即可。

❶ Cut the beef into thin slices and marinate in ② for half an hour. Wash, seed and dice the green pepper. Beat the eggs.

❷ Heat the wok, add 2 T. of oil. Stir fry the green pepper and hot red pepper till done, remove. Heat the wok again, add 3 T. of oil, stir fry the beef to half done, and remove.

❸ Heat the wok, add 1 T. of oil, stir fry ① until fragrant; pour in ③ to boil. Quickly stir in the beef and turn off the fire. Gently mix in the eggs. Thicken with ④. Add green pepper and red pepper, mix evenly and serve.

❶

果汁牛肉串
Tropical Beef Kebabs

6人份 Serves 6

牛排肉⋯⋯⋯⋯⋯250公克
鳳梨（罐頭）⋯⋯100公克
熟紅蘿蔔⋯⋯⋯⋯50公克
青椒⋯⋯⋯⋯⋯⋯40公克
竹串⋯⋯⋯⋯⋯⋯12支

① { 鳳梨汁⋯⋯⋯2大匙
    醬油⋯⋯⋯⋯1½大匙
    酒⋯⋯⋯⋯⋯½大匙

② { 水⋯⋯⋯⋯⋯¼杯
    鳳梨汁⋯⋯⋯4大匙
    醬油⋯⋯⋯⋯2大匙
    糖⋯⋯⋯⋯⋯1½大匙
    油⋯⋯⋯⋯⋯1大匙
    檸檬汁⋯⋯⋯1小匙

250 g. (9 oz.)	beef tenderloin	
100 g. (3½ oz.)	canned whole pineapple	
50 g. (1¾ oz.)	precooked carrots	
40 g. (1½ oz.)	green pepper	
12	bamboo skewers	

①{
2 T.	pineapple juice
1½ T.	soy sauce
½ T.	cooking wine

②{
¼ c.	water
4 T.	pineapple juice
2T.	soy sauce
1½ T.	sugar
1 T.	oil
1 T.	lemon juice

❶ 牛排肉洗淨切3×2公分正方丁，入①料拌勻醃約半小時；鳳梨罐頭開罐後，每片鳳梨切成六等份扇形（圖1）備用。
❷ 紅蘿蔔及青椒均切成2公分方形；②料煮開後，以小火煮至湯汁剩約5大匙，即為果汁烤肉醬，備用。
❸ 將牛肉、鳳梨、青椒及紅蘿蔔以竹串串成串；烤箱預熱至200℃（400°F），將肉串入烤箱邊烤邊刷上煮好的烤肉醬，待肉熟即可（約20分鐘）。

❶ Rinse the beef then cut into 3x2 cm (1⅓" x 1") cubes. Marinate in ① for 30 minutes. Slice the pineapple into pieces(illus. 1).
❷ Cut both carrots and pepper into 3 x 2 cm (1⅓" x 1") cubes, bring ② to a boil, then turn the heat to low. Cook until the liquid reduce to 5 T., this is the fruit Bar-B-Q sauce.
❸ Skewer the beef, pineapple, green pepper into 12 beef kebabs. Preheat the oven to 400°F (200°C). Arrange the beef kebabs in the oven and brush the fruit Bar-B-Q sauce on them several timesduring baking. Remove and serve when it is cooked (about 20 min.).

蘋香牛腩
Apple Flavored Beef

牛腩‥‥‥‥‥‥‥‥‥‥‥300公克
青江菜、蘋果‥‥‥‥‥‥‥各200公克
鹽‥‥‥‥‥‥‥‥‥‥‥‥‥½小匙

① {
水‥‥‥‥‥‥‥‥‥‥‥‥½杯
蕃茄醬‥‥‥‥‥‥‥‥‥2大匙
油、醬油、辣豆瓣醬‥‥‥各1大匙
酒‥‥‥‥‥‥‥‥‥‥‥½大匙
鹽‥‥‥‥‥‥‥‥‥‥‥¼小匙

② {
水‥‥‥‥‥‥‥‥‥‥‥1小匙
太白粉‥‥‥‥‥‥‥‥‥½小匙

300 g. (²/₃ 1b.)		beef brisket
200 g. (¹/₂ 1b.) each		bok choy, apple
¹/₂ t.		salt
①	1.2 c.	water
	2 T.	ketchup
	1 T. each	oil, soy sauce hot soy bean paste
	¹/₄ t.	salt
②	1 t.	water
	¹/₂ t.	corn starch

❶ 青江菜洗淨，以開水燙熟，撈起漂涼；再以1小匙油及½小匙鹽略炒備用。

❷ 牛腩以開水川燙，撈起洗淨，再入他鍋，加水煮開，改小火煮約1小時撈起，待涼切薄片，排至大碗內（圖1）；蘋果去皮去蒂，切小塊置牛腩上（圖2）備用。

❸ 將①料煮開，淋於❷項材料上，入蒸籠大火蒸1小時取出，先倒出蒸汁留用，再倒扣於盤，並以青江菜圍邊備用。

❹ 蒸汁入鍋中煮開，再以②料勾芡，淋於牛腩上即可。

❶ Wash the bok choy, boil till done and remove to cool. Stir fry slightly with 1 t. of oil and ¹/₂ t. of salt.

❷ Parboil the brisket; drain and wash clean. Place the beef in a pot and cover with water. Bring it to boil, reduce the fire to simmer for an hour, remove the meat to cool. When cold, slice it into thin slices. Arrange the slices in a big bowl (illus. 1); place the pared and diced apple on top of the beef (illus. 2).

❸ Bring ① to a boil and pour over ❷. Place it in a steamer and steam over high heat for an hour. Drain the sauce into a small pot, then turn the beef upside down onto a plate; surround the beef with bok choy.

❹ Bring the sauce to a boil and thicken it with ②. Pour over the beef and serve.

三杯茄子
Spicy Eggplant

茄子	600公克
九層塔	100公克
香菜末	3大匙
麻油	1½大匙
① { 薑片	2大匙
蒜片、紅辣椒片	各1大匙
② { 酒、醬油	各¼杯
糖	½大匙

❶ 茄子洗淨去蒂，切約5公分長段；入7分熱(約140℃，280℉)油鍋，炸約4分鐘，撈起瀝油備用。

❷ 取一砂鍋入麻油，再入①料拌炒數下，最後入九層塔、香菜末、茄子及②料，以小火燜煮約5分鐘即可。

---

600 g. (1⅓ 1b.) eggplant
100 g. (3½ oz.) sweet basil
3 T. minced coriander
1½ T. sesame oil
① { 2 T. sliced ginger
1 T. each sliced garlic, sliced hot red pepper
② { ¼ C. each cooking wine, soy sauce
½ T. sugar

❶ Wash the eggplant, discard the stem; and cut into 5 cm (2⅓") long sections. Heat the wok, add 4 C. of oil. Heat the oil to 280°F (140°C), add in the eggplant; fry for 4 minutes. Lift out.

❷ Add the sesame oil into a ceramic pot, stir fry ① for a while; then add in sweet basil, coriander, eggplant and ② . Simmer with lid for 5 minutes and serve.

6人份 Serves 6

6人份 Serves 6

烤鮮洋菇
Fresh Mushrooms in Foil

新鮮洋菇(大)	12個
蒜片	3大匙
奶油	1大匙
鋁箔紙	1張
① { 酒、麻油	各1小匙
鹽	¼小匙
味精、黑胡椒	各少許

❶ 洋菇洗淨去蒂，入①料醃約10分鐘；鍋熱入油1杯，將蒜片炸成金黃色，撈出備用。

❷ 鋁箔紙上置奶油、洋菇及蒜片，包好入150℃(300℉)烤箱，烤約10分鐘即可。

---

12 fresh mushrooms (large)
3 T. sliced garlic
1 T. butter
1 sheet foil
① { 1 t. each cooking wine, sesame oil
¼ t. salt
Dash black pepper

❶ Wash the mushrooms and cut off the stems; marinate in ① for 10 minutes. Heat the wok, add 1 C. of oil, fry the garlic to golden; lift out to use.

❷ Butter the foil, place mushrooms and garlic in it; wrap and close the top opening. Bake in a pre-heated oven 300°F (150°C) for 10 minutes and serve.

雪菜玉筍 (圖左 illus. left)
Bamboo Shoot with Salted Mustard

綠竹筍(淨重) ⋯300公克
雪菜⋯⋯⋯⋯⋯100公克
糖⋯⋯⋯⋯⋯⋯1½大匙

300 g. (²⁄₃ 1b.)　bamboo shoot
100 g. (3½ oz.)　salted mustard
1½ T.　　　　　sugar

❶ 竹筍洗淨，切滾刀塊；雪菜洗淨，擠乾水份備用。
❷ 油4杯燒至6分熱(約120°C，240°F)，入竹筍炸熟，撈起瀝油；再將油燒至
　 7、8分熱，入雪菜炸酥，撈起瀝油備用。
❸ 將油倒出，再入竹筍、雪菜及糖拌勻即可。

❶ Wash bamboo shoot, cut lengthwise into slanting pieces. Rinse the
salted mustard, drain well.
❷ Heat 4 C. of oil in a wok to 240°F (120°C), fry bamboo shoot until
done; lift out and drain off the oil. Heat the oil again to moderate
temperature, add in salted vegetable to crispy, lift out and drain off
the oil.
❸ Pour out the oil, add in again bamboo shoot, salted vegetable and
sugar; mix well and serve.

香葱芋餅 (圖右上 illus. right up)
Aromatic Taro Pancake

❶ 蝦米泡軟瀝乾，剁碎；蛋打散備用。
❷ 芋頭洗淨去皮，刨成細絲，入洋火腿末、蝦米、蛋液、葱末及①料拌勻，分為12等份，每份均做成圓餅狀備用。
❸ 鍋熱入油，燒至7分熱(約140℃，280°F)，入芋餅炸成金黃色即可。

❶ Soak dried shrimp in warm water, drain and chop fine. Beat the egg to use.
❷ Wash and skin the taro, shave to fine shreds; mix in ham, dried shrimp, egg, green onion and ① evenly. Separate it into 12 equal portions; round and flatten them into pancakes.
❸ Heat 6 T. of oil to 280°F (140°C), fry the taro pancakes to golden.

芋頭‥‥‥‥‥‥350公克
羊火腿末‥‥‥‥25公克
蝦米‥‥‥‥‥‥15公克
蛋‥‥‥‥‥‥‥1個
葱末‥‥‥‥‥‥1大匙
① { 太白粉‥‥‥‥2小匙
味精‥‥‥‥½小匙
鹽、糖‥‥‥各¼小匙

350 g. (12⅓ oz.) taro
25 g. (1 oz.) minced ham
15 g. (½ oz.) dried shrimp
1 egg
1 T. minced green onion
① { 2 t. corn starch
¼ each salt, sugar

干貝筍衣 (圖右下 illus. right down)
Bamboo Shoot with Dried Scallop

❶ 綠竹筍先煮熟，再切薄片；干貝加水入蒸籠蒸軟，取出撕成絲備用。
❷ 將筍片、火腿絲、干貝絲及①料煮數分鐘，再以②料勾芡即可。

❶ Boil the bamboo shoot until done, cut into thin slices. Steam the dried scallops with a little water to soften, shred to use.
❷ Bring ①, bamboo shoot, ham, and scallop to boil for a few minutes. Thicken with ② and serve.

綠竹筍(淨重)‥‥‥‥600公克
中式火腿絲‥‥‥‥‥50公克
干貝‥‥‥‥‥‥‥2個
水‥‥‥‥‥‥‥‥½杯
① { 高湯‥‥‥‥‥‥2杯
糖‥‥‥‥‥‥‥½小匙
胡椒粉‥‥‥‥‥少許
② { 水‥‥‥‥‥‥‥1大匙
太白粉‥‥‥‥‥2小匙

600 g. (1⅓ 1b.) (net weight) bamboo shoot
50 g. (1¾ oz.) shredded Chinese ham
2 dried scallops
½ C. water
① { 2 C. stock
½ t. sugar
Dash pepper
② { 1 T. water
2 t. corn starch

6人份 Serves 6

奶油花菜(圖左 illus. left)
Broccoli With Cream Sauce

❶ 花菜洗淨，切成小朵狀並去纖維，入開水燙熟，撈出備用。
❷ ①料煮開，入花菜煮約1分鐘，以②料勾芡，起鍋前撒上洋火腿末即可。

❶ Wash the broccoli and peel off the hard fiber, cut into small sprigs. Boil until done. Drain to use.
❷ Bring ① to boil, add broccoli for 1 minute; thicken with ②. Sprinkle on minced ham before serving.

花菜⋯⋯⋯⋯⋯⋯450公克
洋火腿末⋯⋯⋯⋯10公克
① ⎰ 水⋯⋯⋯⋯⋯1杯
　 ⎪ 奶水⋯⋯⋯⋯3大匙
　 ⎨ 鹽⋯⋯⋯⋯⋯¼小匙
　 ⎩ 糖、味精⋯⋯各1／8小匙
② ⎰ 水⋯⋯⋯⋯⋯1大匙
　 ⎱ 太白粉⋯⋯⋯1小匙

450 g. (1 1b.)　broccoli
10 g. (¹/₃ oz.)　minced ham
① ⎰ 1 C.　water
　 ⎪ 3 T.　milk
　 ⎨ ¹/₄ t.　salt
　 ⎩ ¹/₈ t.　sugar
② ⎰ 1 T.　water
　 ⎱ 1 t.　corn starch

四季紅絲 （圖右上 illus. right up）
Colorful Shredded Chicken

❶ 四季豆洗淨切細絲，入開水川燙2分鐘，取出漂涼；雞胸肉切細絲，入①料拌勻備用。
❷ 鍋熱入油3大匙，續入雞絲炒熟取出；餘油再熱，入四季豆、紅蘿蔔炒片刻，隨入②料及雞絲拌勻即可。

❶ Wash and shred the string bean; boil in hot water for 2 minutes, drain and cool. Shred the chicken breast and marinate in ①.
❷ Heat the wok, add 3 T. of oil. Stir fry the chicken until done, lift out. Heat the remaining oil again, add in string bean, carrot for a while; mix in salt and chicken evenly. Serve.

四季豆⋯⋯⋯⋯⋯⋯200公克
雞胸肉、熟紅蘿蔔絲⋯⋯各100公克

① {
水⋯⋯⋯⋯⋯1大匙
太白粉⋯⋯⋯1小匙
酒、醬油⋯⋯各½小匙
鹽、味精⋯⋯各⅛小匙
}

② {
鹽⋯⋯⋯⋯⋯½小匙
味精⋯⋯⋯⋯¼小匙
}

200 g. (7 oz.)
    string bean
100 g. (3½ oz.) each
    chicken breast,
    cooked and shredded carrot

① {
1 T.   water
1 t.   corn starch
½ t. each   cooking wine, soy sauce
⅛ t.   salt
}
½ t.   salt

莧菜羹 （圖右下 illus. right down）
Amaranth Potage

❶ 莧菜洗淨，切3公分長段；魩仔魚洗淨，瀝乾水分備用。
❷ 鍋熱入油，爆香蒜末，入魩仔魚炒香，續入莧菜炒勻，再入①料，燜煮至莧菜熟爛，以②料勾芡即可。

❶ Wash the amaranth, cut into 3 cm (1⅓") long sections. Wash the small fish and drain.
❷ Heat the wok, add 3 T. of oil. Stir fry the gorlic until fragrant, add the small fish; then add in amaranth evenly. Mix in ①. Simmer until amaranth is tender, thicken with ② and serve.

莧菜⋯⋯⋯⋯⋯⋯400公克
魩仔魚⋯⋯⋯⋯⋯50公克
蒜末⋯⋯⋯⋯⋯1½大匙

① {
水⋯⋯⋯⋯⋯2½杯
酒⋯⋯⋯⋯⋯1小匙
味精⋯⋯⋯⋯½小匙
鹽⋯⋯⋯⋯⋯⅜小匙
}

② {
水⋯⋯⋯⋯⋯1大匙
太白粉⋯⋯⋯1½小匙
}

400 g. (14 oz.) amaranth
50 g. (1¾ oz.) small fish
1½ T.   minced garlic

① {
2½ C. water
1 t.   cooking wine
⅜ t.   salt
}

② {
1 T.   water
1½ t. corn starch
}

6人份 Serves 6

糖醋白蘿蔔 (圖左 illus. left)
Sweet and Sour Turnip

白蘿蔔……600公克
紅辣椒……1枝
花椒粒……1小匙
鹽…………½小匙
① { 醋……3大匙
    糖……2大匙

600 g. (1⅓ 1b.) turnip
1   hot red pepper
1 t.   peppercorns
½ t.   salt
① { 3 T. vinegar
    2 T. sugar

❶ 白蘿蔔以刨絲器刨成薄片，入鹽略醃使白蘿蔔變軟；紅辣椒洗淨切絲狀備用。
❷ 用冷開水洗去白蘿蔔鹽分，再和紅辣椒絲、花椒粒及①料拌勻，醃至入味即可。

❶ Shave turnip into thin slices with a shredder, marinate turnip slices slightly with salt to soften. Wash and shred hot red pepper to use.
❷ Wash the salt off turnip with cold water; mix with hot red pepper, peppercorns and ① evenly, marinate until turnip becomes tasty.

靑豆泥（圖右上 illus. right up）
Peas Puree

❶ 靑豆加½杯水用果汁機打成泥；豆腐切丁備用。
❷ 高湯煮開，放入豆腐及洋菇煮開後，續入靑豆略煮，以①料勾芡，再入蝦仁及②料煮開，蛋白打散徐徐加入湯內即可。

❶ Puree the peas and $1/2$ c. of water in a blender. Dice the bean curd.
❷ Bring the stock to a boil, add bean curd and mushrooms. Mix in peas. When boiling again; thicken with ①. Add shrimps and salt. Bring to boil again, beat the egg white lightly and pour in the soup slowly. Serve.

靑豆（罐頭或冷凍）220公克
小蝦仁、洋菇丁……各70公克
豆腐…………………½塊
蛋白…………………2個
高湯…………………4杯
① { 水、太白粉……各1大匙
② { 鹽……………………⅔小匙
    味精…………………½小匙

220 g. ($7^2/_3$ oz.)	canned or frozen peas	
70 g. ($2^1/_2$ oz.)	shelled small shrimps, diced mushrooms	
$1/2$	bean curd	
2	egg whites	
4 c.	stock	
① {	1 T. each	water, corn starch
	$2/3$ t.	salt

銀芽蛋皮（圖右下 illus. right down）
Silvery Bean Sprout with Golden Egg

❶ 韭菜洗淨，切4公分長段；蛋打散備用。
❷ 鍋熱入油1大匙，倒入蛋液，以小火煎成蛋皮，切4×0.5公分長段備用。
❸ 鍋熱入油1½大匙，入銀芽及紅蘿蔔絲略炒，隨入韭菜及①料，最後入蛋絲拌勻即可。

❶ Wash the chive, cut into 4 cm ($1^3/_4$") sections. Beat the egg to use.
❷ Heat the wok, add 1 T. of oil. Pour in the beatened egg, swing the wok gently over low fire to make egg crepe. Cut into 4 x 0.5 cm ($1^3/_4$" x $1/_4$") long strips.
❸ Heat the wok, add $1^1/_2$ T. of oil. Stir fry bean sprout and carrot; add in chive add ①. Finally mix in egg strips evenly and serve.

銀芽…………300公克
韭菜…………120公克
熟紅蘿蔔絲……10公克
蛋………………1個
① { 鹽…………½小匙
    味精…………$1/_8$小匙
    胡椒粉……少許

300 g. ($2/3$ 1b.)	bean sprout	
120 g. (4 $1/4$ oz.)	yellow chive	
10 g. ($1/3$ oz.)	cooked and shredded carrot	
1	egg	
① {	$1/2$ t.	salt
	Dash	pepper

6人份 Serves 6

酥炸葫蘆（圖左上 illus. left up）
Crispy Squash

❶ 葫瓜去皮，切條狀；①料拌勻成麵糊備用。
❷ 將葫瓜條沾裹麵糊，入7分熱（約140℃，280℉）油鍋，炸至稍黃撈起；再開大火將油燒熱，再入葫瓜條迅速炸至金黃即可。食時可沾胡椒鹽。

❶ Skin the squash, cut into long strips. Mix ① well into paste.
❷ Dip squash strips into the paste. Heat 6 C. of oil in the wok to 280°F (140°C); deep fry the squash until golden, lift out. Heat the oil again before adding the second batch. Serve with pepper salt.

葫瓜	…………	370公克
胡椒鹽	………	1小匙

① ⎰ 麵粉……⅔杯
   ⎱ 水………½杯
   ⎱ 油………1大匙
   ⎱ 發粉……⅔小匙

370 g. (13 oz.)　squash
1 t.　　　　　　pepper salt

① ⎰ ⅔ C.　flour
   ⎱ ½ C.　water
   ⎱ 1 T.　oil
   ⎱ ⅔ t.　baking pawder

茄子炒九層塔 <small>(圖右 illus. right)</small>
Eggplant With Sweet Basil

❶ 九層塔取嫩葉；茄子洗淨，由中間剖開，切約0.5公分寬的長條，泡水備用。

❷ 鍋熱入油，爆香①料，入茄子炒軟，續入②料及九層塔拌勻，起鍋前灑上麻油即可。

❶ Use the young top leaves of sweet basil only. Wash the eggplant, cut lengthwise in the middle into 0.5 cm ($1/4$") wide long strips; soak in water.

❷ Heat the wok, add 3 T. of oil. Stir fry ① until fragrant; add in drained eggplant until softened. Continue adding in ② and sweet basil, mix evenly. Sprinkle on sesame oil before serving.

茄子·······················450公克
九層塔·················30公克
麻油·······················少許
①蒜末、辣椒末···各1小匙
② 醬油膏···········2大匙
糖················1 ½大匙
醋················1大匙
味精·············¼小匙
鹽·············½小匙

450 g. (1 lb.) eggplant
30 g. (1 oz.) sweet basil
Dash sesame oil
① { 1 t. each minced garlic,
          minced hot red pepper
② { 2 T. soy sauce
     1½ T. sugar
     1 T. vinegar
     ½ t. salt

蟹肉白菜 <small>(圖下 illus. down)</small>
Cabbage With Crab Meat

❶ 白菜洗淨切塊，入開水川燙備用。

❷ 鍋熱入油3大匙爆香薑片，續入白菜及①料煮至菜軟，加入蟹肉拌勻，以②料勾芡即可。

❶ Wash the cabbage, cut into desired pieces. Parboil and drain.

❷ Heat the wok, add 3 T. of oil. Stir fry the ginger until fragrant, add in the cabbage and ①; cook until the cabbage is tender. Mix in the crab meat, thicken with ② and serve.

白菜·······················600公克
薑片·······················3片
蟹肉·······················½杯
① 高湯·············1杯
酒················½大匙
鹽················¾小匙
麻油·············少許
② 水、太白粉······各1½大匙

600 g. (1⅓ lb.) Chinese cabbage
3 slices ginger
½ C. crab meat
① { 1 C. stock
     ½ T. cooking wine
     ¾ t. salt
     few drops sesame oil
② 1½ T. each water, corn starch

高麗髮菜
Braised Cabbage with Black Moss

高麗菜‥‥‥‥‥‥‥300公克
髮菜(圖1)‥‥‥‥‥12公克
干貝‥‥‥‥‥‥‥‥2個
葱段‥‥‥‥‥‥‥‥6段
水‥‥‥‥‥‥‥‥‥4大匙
蒜末‥‥‥‥‥‥‥‥1小匙
① { 鹽‥‥‥‥‥‥‥‥¼小匙
   味精‥‥‥‥‥‥‥少許
② { 水‥‥‥‥‥‥‥‥3大匙
   糖‥‥‥‥‥‥‥‥½小匙
   鹽‥‥‥‥‥‥‥‥⅛小匙
   麻油‥‥‥‥‥‥‥少許
③ 水、太白粉‥‥‥各1小匙

300 g. (²/₃ 1b.)	cabbage	
12 g. (¹/₂ oz.)	black moss (illus. 1)	
2	dried scallops	
6 sections	green onion	
4 T.	water	
1 t.	minceded garlic	
① ¼ t.	salt	
② { 3 T.	water	
¹/₂ t.	sugar	
¹/₈ t.	salt	
Dash	sesame oil	
③ 1 t. each	water, corn starch	

❶ 高麗菜洗淨切塊,髮菜泡水洗淨瀝乾,干貝以水煮軟撕成絲,干貝汁留著備用。
❷ 鍋熱入油2大匙爆香蒜末,入高麗菜及①料炒熟,取出備用。
❸ 鍋熱入油1大匙爆香葱段,再入髮菜、干貝絲、②料及高麗菜拌勻,燜煮2分鐘後取出盛盤;餘汁以③料勾芡,再淋在高麗菜上即可。

❶ Wash and cut cabbage into pieces; soak the black moss briefly in water, then rinse clean and drain. Steam dried scallops with water to soften and shred. Keep the scallop juice for sauce.
❷ Heat the wok, and 2 T. of oil. Stir fry minced garlic until fragrant; add in cabbage and ① until done. Remove.
❸ Heat the wok, add 1 T. of oil. Stir fry green onion until fragrant; add black moss, shredded scallop, and ②, mix thoroughly with cabbage and braise covered for 2 minutes. Remove onto a plate. Thicken all the juice with ③; pour over the cabbage and serve.

白玉鑲肉
Jaded Pork

冬瓜·····················300公克
絞肉·····················60公克
太白粉·····················1½大匙
水·····················1大匙
麻油、香菜·····················各少許

① 花瓜末·····················3大匙
　 蛋液·····················½大匙
　 花瓜汁、太白粉·····各1小匙
　 葱末、薑末·········各⅓小匙
　 鹽、味精、胡椒粉···各少許

② 醬油·····················1大匙
　 酒、花瓜汁·········各½大匙
　 糖·····················½小匙
　 味精、胡椒粉········各少許

300 g. (²⁄₃ 1b.)　winter melon
60 g. (2 oz.)　　grounded pork
1½ T.　　　　　corn starch
1 T.　　　　　　water
a little each　　sesame oil,
　　　　　　　　coriander

① 　3 T.　　minced Chinese
　　　　　　pickled cucumbers
　　½ T.　　beatened egg
　　1 t. each　corn starch, juice
　　　　　　from the Chinses
　　　　　　pickled cucumber
　　⅓ t. each　minced green onion,
　　　　　　minced ginger
　　Dash　　salt, pepper

② 　1 T.　　soy sauce
　　½ T. each　cooking wine, juice
　　　　　　from the Chinese
　　　　　　pickled cucumber
　　½ t.　　sugar
　　Dash　　pepper

❶ 絞肉加①料拌勻，醃約10分鐘；太白粉½大匙加水1大匙調勻備用。

❷ 冬瓜去皮切成2公分厚之扇形6大塊，中間劃開一刀（圖1），抹上乾太白粉，夾入絞肉（圖2），置於盤上，入蒸籠以中火蒸約30分鐘（直至冬瓜顏色變成透明）取出。

❸ 倒出蒸汁加②料入鍋煮開，以太白粉水勾芡，灑上麻油，再淋在冬瓜夾上，並以香菜葉裝飾即可。

❶ Marinate the pork with ① for 10 minutes. Mix ½ T. of corn starch with 1 T. of water to use.

❷ Skin the winter melon; cut it into 6 fan-shaped large pieces with 2 cm (1") thickness. Slit the pieces in the middle (illus. 1), dust on dry corn starch, stuff the pork into the pockets (illus. 2). Place them on a plate and steam in a steamer about 30 minutes (until winter melon turns transparent), remove.

❸ Pour out the sauce, add in ②; bring it to a boil, and thicken with corn starch mixed with water. Sprinkle sesame oil on the sauce. Pour over winter melon and decorate with coriander.

69

6人份 Serves 6

芙蓉筍 (圖左 illus. left)
Bamboo Fu-Yung

綠竹筍(切絲)	400公克
韮黃	35公克
蛋	3個
鹽	½小匙
① { 鹽	½小匙
味精、胡椒粉	各¼小匙

400 g. (14 oz.)	cooked and shredded bamboo shoot
35 g. (1¼ oz.)	yellow chive
3	eggs
½ t.	salt
① { ½ t.	salt
Dash	pepper

❶ 韮黃洗淨切段；蛋打散，加½小匙鹽拌勻備用。
❷ 鍋熱入油4大匙，續入筍絲略炒，再入韮黃及①料拌勻，後入蛋液炒至凝固即可。

❶ Wash the yellow chive and cut into sections. Beat the eggs with ½ t. of salt to use.
❷ Heat the wok, add 4 T. of oil. Stir fry the bamboo shoot slightly, add in yellow chive and ① evenly; finally add in the eggs. Fry until the eggs hardened and serve.

魚肉豆腐 (圖右上 illus. right up)
Bean Curd With Fish

❶ 魚肉切片，以①料略醃，豆腐切成3×3×1公分塊狀備用。
❷ 鍋熱入油3大匙，將豆腐兩面煎黃，入②料煮開，再入魚肉煮熟，以③料勾芡，撒上葱末即可。

❶ Slice the fish fillet, marinate with ①. Cut the bean curds into 3 x 3 x 1 cm (1$^1/_3$" x 1$^1/_3$" x $^1/_2$") cubes to use.
❷ Heat the wok, add 3 T. of oil; fry the bean curds to golden on both sides. Add in ②, cook until boil; add fish, cook until done. Thicken with ③; sprinkle on minced green onion before serving.

魚肉‥‥‥‥‥‥‥‥‥110公克
豆腐‥‥‥‥‥‥‥‥‥2塊
葱末‥‥‥‥‥‥‥‥‥2大匙

① { 酒‥‥‥‥‥‥‥1小匙
    鹽‥‥‥‥‥‥‥¼小匙

② { 高湯‥‥‥‥‥‥1½杯
    鹽、味精‥‥‥‥各1小匙
    胡椒粉‥‥‥‥‥少許

③ 水、太白粉‥‥‥各1大匙

110 g. (4 oz.) fish fillet
2 blocks   bean curd
2 T.   minced green onion
① { 1 t.   cooking wine
    ¼ t.   salt
② { 1½ C. stock
    1 t.   salt
    Dash   pepper
③ 1 T. each water, corn starch

玉米醬燒豆腐 (圖右下 illus. right down)
Corn Braised Bean Curd

❶ 豆腐每塊對切成半，再切成2×1公分小塊，加鹽醃15分鐘；蛋黃入玉米醬拌勻備用。
❷ 鍋熱入油3大匙，將豆腐略煎，入①料及玉米醬，以小火燜煮2分鐘，起鍋前拌入②料即可。

❶ Cut the bean curds to half, again cut into 2 x 1 cm (1" x $^1/_2$") small cubes; marinate with salt for 15 minutes. Mix egg yolk to cream of corn evenly, to use.
❷ Heat the wok, add 3 T. of oil. Fry the bean curd slightly, add ① and cream of corn; cook over low heat for 2 minutes. Mix in ② before serving.

豆腐‥‥‥‥‥‥‥‥‥2塊
玉米醬罐頭‥‥‥‥‥‥½罐
蛋黃‥‥‥‥‥‥‥‥‥1個
鹽‥‥‥‥‥‥‥‥‥‥½小匙

① { 高湯‥‥‥‥‥‥½杯
    鹽、胡椒粉‥‥‥各⅛小匙
    麻油‥‥‥‥‥‥少許

② 葱末、火腿末‥‥各1大匙

2 blocks bean curds
½ can   cream of corn
1   egg yolk
½ t.   salt
① { ½ C.   stock
    ⅛ t. each salt, pepper
    few drops sesame oil
② 1 T. each   minced green onion,
              minced ham

6人份 Serves 6

蒜泥蒸蛋（圖左 illus. left）
Egg Custard With Garlic

蛋⋯⋯⋯⋯⋯⋯⋯3個
蒜泥⋯⋯⋯⋯⋯⋯2大匙
葱末⋯⋯⋯⋯⋯⋯1小匙
① ⎰ 高湯（或水）⋯⋯1¾杯
　 ⎱ 鹽⋯⋯⋯⋯⋯⋯¾小匙
　 　 味精⋯⋯⋯⋯⋯¼小匙

3　 eggs
2 T.　mashed garlic
1 t.　minced green onion
① ⎰ 1¾ C.　stock (or water)
　 ⎱ ¾ t.　　salt

❶ 蛋打散，加蒜泥拌勻，再緩緩加入①料中拌勻；以小火蒸20分鐘即可；食時撒上葱末即可。

■ 蒜泥份量可依個人喜好酌量增減。

■ 高湯應等涼了再用，蛋加入時動作應慢，並輕輕拌勻，否則會形成蛋花。

❶ Beat the eggs slightly and add mashed garlic; gradually mix in ① evenly. Steam over low heat for 20 minutes. Sprinkle minced green onion on top and serve.

■ Quantity of mashed garlic depends on personal taste.

■ Stock should be cold when use. Eggs should be added in slowly and mix gently after each addition; or eggs would harden too fast and would not form to be a custard.

蟹肉豆腐 (圖上 illus. up)
Bean Curd with Crab Meat

❶ 豆腐切1公分立方塊；③料拌勻備用。
❷ 鍋熱入油2大匙爆香葱、薑，隨入蟹肉及酒拌炒數下，再入①料及豆腐，中火煮約3分鐘，以②料勾芡後徐徐加入③料即可。

❶ Cut the bean curd into 1 cm (½") cubes. Mix ③ to use.
❷ Heat the wok, add 2 T. oil; stir fry green onion and ginger until fragrant. Stir in crab meat and cooking wine, fry for a few seconds. Then add in ① and bean curd, cook over medium heat for 3 minutes. Thicken with ②; slowly pour in ③ and serve.

蟹肉······················½杯
豆腐······················1塊
葱末、薑末············各1大匙
酒························½大匙
① ┌ 高湯················1杯
   │ 鹽·················½小匙
   │ 麻油、胡椒粉······各¼小匙
   └ 味精···············少許
② 水、太白粉···········各½大匙
③ ┌ 蛋白···············1個
   └ 水·················1大匙

½ C.   crab meat
1   bean curd
1 T. each minced green onion,
           minced ginger
½ T.   cooking wine
① ┌ 1 C.   stock
   │ ½ t.   salt
   └ ¼ t. each sesame oil, pepper
② ½ T. each water, corn starch
③ ┌ 1   egg white
   └ 1 T.   water

韭菜豆干 (圖右下 illus. right down)
Chive and Dried Bean Curd Salad

❶ 韭菜洗淨，以開水燙熟，取出切細末狀備用。
❷ 白豆干切小丁，以開水煮熟，撈出備用。
❸ 將韭菜、白豆干及①料拌勻即可。

❶ Wash the chive, boil until done and mince.
❷ Dice the white pressed bean curd, boil until done and drain.
❸ Mix the chive, pressed bean curd, and stir ① thoroughly and serve.

韭菜············150公克
白豆干··········140公克
① ┌ 麻油·······1大匙
   │ 鹽·········½小匙
   └ 味精·······¼小匙

150 g. (⅓ 1b.) chive
140 g. (5 oz.)   white pressed
                 bean curd
① ┌ 1 T.   sesame oil
   └ ½ t. salt

毛豆豆干 (圖左 illus. left)
Vegetarian Platter

毛豆、豆干⋯⋯⋯⋯各 150 公 克

① ⎰ 糖、醬油⋯⋯⋯各1大匙
　⎨ 鹽⋯⋯⋯⋯⋯⋯⋯½小匙
　⎱ 味精⋯⋯⋯⋯⋯⋯¼小匙

150 g. (⅓ 1b.) each
　　fresh soybeans or peas,
　　pressed bean curds

① ⎰ 1 T. each sugar, soy sauce
　⎱ ½ t.　　　salt

❶ 毛豆洗淨瀝乾，豆干切小丁備用。
❷ 鍋熱入油3大匙，入毛豆、豆干丁及①料拌炒至熟即可。

❶ Wash the fresh soybeans and drain. Dice the pressed bean curds.
❷ Heat the wok, and add 3 T. of oil, stir fry fresh soybeans, pressed bean curds and ① until cooked. Remove and serve.

五香辣豆（圖右上 illus. right up）
Hot Five-spiced Soybeans

❶ 黃豆浸泡一夜，撈起瀝乾備用。
❷ 鍋熱入油，將黃豆拌炒片刻，續入①料燜煮30分鐘，待黃豆全部燜爛為止，再入麻油、紅辣椒末，炒至湯汁收乾即可。

❶ Soak the soybeans overnight, drain.
❷ Heat the wok, add 2 T. of oil. Stir fry the soybeans for a while, add ① to braise for 30 minutes until the soybean is very tender. Add in sesame oil and hot red pepper, fry until all the juice is soaked dry. Serve.

黃豆·················150公克
紅辣椒末、麻油······各1大匙
① 水·················1½杯
　 鹽·················¾小匙
　 五香粉·············½小匙
　 味精·············¼小匙

150 g. (⅓ 1b.) soybeans
1 T. each　　hot red pepper
　　　　　　powder, sesame oil
① 1½ C.　water
　 ¾ t.　　salt
　 ½ t.　　five spice powder

百頁雪菜（圖右下 illus. right down）
Bean Curd Sheet With Greens

❶ 百頁以①料泡約10分鐘，呈白色軟化時，取出沖冷水去鹼味，再切成3×3公分片狀；雪菜洗淨切末備用。
❷ 鍋熱入油2大匙，續入雪菜略炒，隨入百頁及②料煮熟，以③料勾芡即可。
■ ①料中之鹼粉也可以蘇打粉代替。

❶ Soak bean curd sheets in ① for 10 minutes until whitened and softened; lift out and rinse under cold water. Then cut them into 3 x 3 cm (1⅓" x 1⅓") slices. Rinse the salted mustard and drain, then mince to use.
❷ Heat the wok, add 2 T. of oil. Stir fry the salted vegetable for a while, add in bean curd sheet and ②. Thicken with ③ and serve.

百頁·················10張
雪菜·················110公克
① 水·················6杯
　 鹼粉·············½大匙
② 高湯·············1½杯
　 鹽·················⅔小匙
　 味精·············½小匙
③ 水、太白粉······各1大匙

10　　　　　　bean curd sheets
110 g. (4 oz.)　salted mustard
① 6 C.　　water
　 ½ T.　　baking soda
② 1½ C.　stock
　 ⅔ t.　　salt
③ 1 T. each　water, corn starch

三鮮蒸蛋
Seafood Egg Custard

蛤蜊……………60公克
蝦仁……………35公克
香菇……………2朵
蛋………………3個
① { 鹽、薑末……¼小匙
    味精…………少許

60 g. (2 oz.) clam
35 g. (1¼ oz.) shelled shrimp
2　　dried black mushrooms
① { 3　　　eggs
    ¼ t. each salt, minced ginger

❶ 2杯水煮沸，入吐過沙之蛤蜊，以小火煮至蛤蜊微開，撈出置中碗內（圖1）；留湯汁½杯待涼。
❷ 香菇泡軟去蒂切絲；蝦仁去腸泥備用。
❸ ①料打散，入1杯水及蛤蜊湯汁，過濾後倒進裝有蛤蜊之中碗內（圖2），置蒸籠內以小火蒸約5分鐘，至蛋稍凝固時輕置蝦仁及香菇於其上，續蒸5分鐘至蝦仁熟即可。

❶ Bring 2 C. of water to a boil, add in sanded clam (see page 8), cook until clams slightly open; lift and place in a bowl (illus. 1). Keep ½ C of the juice to cool.

❷ Soak dried black mushrooms in hot water to soften; discard the stems and shred. Wash and devein the shrimp to use.

❸ Beat ① slightly, add 1 C. of water and clam juice; sieve and pour into the bowl with clams (illus. 2). Steam over low heat for 5 minutes. When the egg is slightly hardened, gently place shrimp and mushroom on top. Continue to steam for another 5 minutes until the shrimp is cooked. Serve hot.

翡翠豆腐
Green-Jaded Bean Curd

6人份 Serves 6

菠菜⋯⋯⋯⋯⋯⋯⋯⋯220公克
香菇⋯⋯⋯⋯⋯⋯⋯⋯⋯3朵
豆腐⋯⋯⋯⋯⋯⋯⋯⋯2大塊
麻油⋯⋯⋯⋯⋯⋯⋯⋯1大匙
① 蛋白⋯⋯⋯⋯⋯⋯⋯2個
　 糖⋯⋯⋯⋯⋯⋯⋯½大匙
　 麻油⋯⋯⋯⋯⋯⋯1小匙
　 鹽、味精、胡椒粉⋯⋯各½小匙
② 高湯（或水）⋯⋯⋯2杯
　 鹽⋯⋯⋯⋯⋯⋯⋯¼小匙
③ 水、太白粉⋯⋯⋯⋯各1大匙

220 g. (7²/₃ oz.) spinach
3　　　　　　 dried black
　　　　　　 mushrooms
2 large blocks bean curds
1 T.　　　　 sesame oil
① 　2　　　　 egg whites
　 ½ T.　　　 sugar
　 1 t.　　　 sesame oil
　 ½ t. each salt, pepper
② 2 C. stock (or water)
　 ¼ t. salt
③ 1 T. each water, corn starch

❶ 菠菜取葉（圖1）（莖不用，淨重約70公克），切碎；豆腐去硬邊（圖2）、壓碎，加入菠菜及①料拌勻成豆腐泥；香菇泡軟去蒂、切末備用。
❷ 備1只中碗，碗底塗麻油，倒入豆腐泥，以中火蒸20分鐘，用筷子插入豆腐，不沾筷子即熟，隨後反扣於盤備用。
❸ 香菇末及②料燒開，以③料勾芡，淋在豆腐上即可。

❶ Discard the stems, use only the spinach leaves to chop fine. (illus. 1) (leaves only net weight 70 g. or 2 1/2 oz.). Cut off the hard edges of bean curds (illus. 2); mash, add in spinach and ①. Mix well to make bean curd mash. Soften the black mushrooms in hot water, cut off the stems and chop fine.
❷ Oil the bottom of a medium sized bowl with sesame oil. Pour in the bean curd mash; steam over medium heat for 20 minutes. Pierce the bean curd with a chop stick, the bean curd is done when it does not stick to chop stick. Turn it upside down onto a plate.
❸ Bring ② and fine chopped black mushrooms to boil, thicken with ③. Pour over the bean curd and serve.

和菜戴帽
Mixed Vegetables With Egg Hat

豆芽、菠菜、里肌肉
·················各110公克
韭黃(圖1) ······75公克
粉絲·············60公克
蛋················2個
葱段············6段

① ┌ 水···········1大匙
  │ 醬油········½大匙
  │ 太白粉······1小匙
  └ 酒··········½小匙

② ┌ 高湯·······1杯
  │ 醬油········1大匙
  └ 鹽··········½小匙

③ ┌ 水···········½大匙
  │ 太白粉······1小匙
  └ 鹽··········⅛小匙

110 g. (4 oz.) each bean sprout,
                     spinach pork loin
75 g. (2⅔ oz.) yellow chive (illus. 1)
60 g. (2 oz.) dried bean thread
2   eggs
6 sections   green onion

① ┌ 1 T. water
  │ ½ T. soy sauce
  │ 1 t. corn starch
  └ ½ t. cooking wine

② ┌ 1 C. stock
  │ 1 T. soy sauce
  └ ½ t. salt

③ ┌ ½ T. water
  │ 1 t. corn starch
  └ ⅛ t. salt

❶

❶ 里肌肉切絲入①料拌勻醃約10分鐘，下鍋前拌入1大匙油。
❷ 粉絲泡軟並切斷；韭黃、菠菜洗淨後切3公分長段；蛋打散入已拌勻的③料備用。
❸ 鍋熱入油3大匙，炒熟肉絲撈出，餘油入韭黃拌炒數下，再入菠菜炒熟撈出備用。
❹ 鍋熱入油1大匙，爆香葱段，入粉絲及②料煮至汁收乾，續入豆芽拌炒數下，再入3項材料拌勻盛盤備用。
❺ 以平底鍋入油1小匙，並用刷子在鍋子中抹勻，再倒入蛋液煎成蛋皮，取出覆蓋在4項材料上即可。

■ 此道菜可以荷葉餅、木須皮或春捲皮包捲而食。

❶ Shred the pork and marinate in ① for 10 minutes; mix in 1 T. of oil befor cooking.
❷ Soak dried bean thread in warm water to soften and cut into shorter sections. Wash chive and spinach, cut into 3 cm (1⅓") long sections. Beat the eggs with ③ to use.
❸ Heat the wok, add 3 T. of oil. Stir fry the pork; lift and remove. Add chives in the remaining oil for a while; continue add in spinach until done and remove.
❹ Heat the wok, add 1 T. of oil. Stir fry the green onion until fragrant; add bean thread and ② until the sauce dries up, then add in bean sprout for a while. Mix in ③ evenly and remove onto a plate.
❺ Heat a flat frying pan, brush 1 t. of oil evenly on the pan. Pour in egg to make a egg crepe. Turn it over ④ as a hat and serve.

■ May be served with mandarin pancakes, Ma Shu pancakes or rolled in spring roll skins.

瓊山豆腐
Egg Bean Curd with Dried Scallops

蛋白‥‥‥‥‥‥‥‥6個
干貝‥‥‥‥‥‥‥‥3個
嫩薑絲‥‥‥‥‥‥‥1大匙
蒜油‥‥‥‥‥‥‥‥少許
水‥‥‥‥‥‥‥‥‥½杯

① ┌ 高湯‥‥‥‥‥‥1杯
　├ 雞油‥‥‥‥‥‥½大匙
　├ 鹽‥‥‥‥‥‥‥¼小匙
　└ 味精‥‥‥‥‥‥少許

② ┌ 高湯‥‥‥‥‥‥1½杯
　├ 鹽‥‥‥‥‥‥‥¼小匙
　├ 酒、味精、
　└ 胡椒粉‥‥‥‥‥各少許

③ 　水、太白粉‥‥‥各1大匙

6　egg whites
3　dried scallops
1 T.　shredded young ginger
Dash　sesame oil
½ C.　water

① ┌ 1 C.　stock
　┤ ½ T.　chicken lard
　└ ¼ t.　salt

② ┌ 1½ C.　　stock
　┤ ¼ t.　　salt
　└ dash each　pepper, cooking wine

③ 1 T. each　water, corn starch

❶ 干貝加水蒸軟，撕成絲（圖1），蒸汁留¼杯備用。
❷ 蛋白加①料及干貝蒸汁拌勻，以篩網過篩（圖2），倒入深盤中入蒸籠，先以大火蒸2分鐘，再以小火蒸約8分鐘，待呈凝固狀取出，上置嫩薑絲備用。
❸ 將②料及干貝絲煮開，以③料勾芡，起鍋前灑上麻油，再淋於蒸好的蛋上即可。

❶ Steam dried scallops with water to soften, tear it to shreds (illus. 1). Keep ¼ C. of juice for sauce.
❷ Mix egg whites with ① and scallop juice thoroughly; pour into a deep plate through a sieve (illus. 2). Steam over high heat for 2 minutes, then reduce to low heat for about 8 minutes. Remove when hardened; place ginger on top.
❸ Bring ② and shredded scallop to boil, thicken with ③. Sprinkle sesame oil before remove. Pour over the egg and serve.

雞扒豆腐
Fast Grip Bean Curd

絞肉⋯⋯⋯⋯100公克
豆腐⋯⋯⋯⋯1塊
蒜苗⋯⋯⋯⋯1隻
① 蝦米(切碎)、葱末、薑末
　　、榨菜末⋯各4大匙
　　水⋯⋯⋯⋯½杯
② 酒⋯⋯⋯⋯1大匙
　　醬油⋯⋯⋯½大匙
　　鹽⋯⋯⋯⋯¼小匙
　　味精⋯⋯⋯少許
③ 水⋯⋯⋯⋯1½小匙
　　太白粉⋯⋯1小匙

100 g. (3½ oz.)　grounded pork
1　　　　　　　bean curd
1 stalk　　　　garlic leek
① 4 T. each
　　minced dried shrimp, minced
　　green onion, minced ginger,
　　minced szechuan pickled
　　mustard green
② ½ C.　water
　　1 T.　cooking wine
　　½ T.　soy sauce
　　¼ t.　salt
③ 1½ t.　water
　　1 t.　corn starch

❶ 豆腐切1公分立方塊，蒜苗切斜片 （圖1）。
❷ 鍋熱入油2大匙，爆香①料，入絞肉拌勻後再入②料及豆腐，煮沸後改小
　火燜煮5分鐘，以③料勾芡，撒上蒜苗拌勻即可。

❶ Cut bean curd into 1 cm (½") cubes; cut garlic leek into slanting slices (illus. 1).
❷ Heat the wok, and 2 T. of oil. Stir fry ① until fragrant. Mix in pork evenly, then add ② and bean curd. When boil, reduce the heat to simmer with lid for 5 minutes. Thicken with ③. Sprinkle on garlic leek and mix evenly. Remove and serve.

鍋塌蛋豆腐
Bean Curd With Egg Coating

豆腐…………1½塊
蛋…………2個
葱末…………1大匙

① 水………¼杯
  醬油……½大匙
  糖………¼大匙

② 醬油……1½大匙
  蒜泥……1大匙

½ block | bean curds
         | eggs
T. | minced green onion

① ¼ C. water
  ½ T. soy sauce
  ¼ T. sugar

② 1½ T. soy sauce
  1 T. mashed garlic

❶ 豆腐切1.5公分厚片，共12片，以乾布吸乾水分（圖1）；蛋打散備用。
❷ 將①料煮開，入葱末拌勻；②料調勻備用。
❸ 鍋熱入油2大匙，再入豆腐煎至兩面金黃，淋下蛋液（圖2）立即翻面，略煎至蛋皮形成，另一面亦以同法煎，如此反覆3次。
❹ 食時沾①料或②料即可。

❶ Cut the bean curd into 1.5 cm ($^3/_4$") thick slices, 12 pieces in total; pat dry with a cloth (illus. 1). Beat the eggs.
❷ Bring ① to a boil, add in minced green onion and mix evenly. Mix ② thoroughly for alternative sauce.
❸ Heat the wok, add 2 T. of oil. Fry the bean curds to golden on bothsides; pour a little egg on top of one side (illus. 2) and turn immediately. Fry until an egg coating is formed. Do the same on the other side of the bean curd. Repeat the process 3 times.
❹ Served with ① sauce or ② sauce.

金茸肉絲湯 (圖左 illus. left)
Golden Mushrooms and Pork Consommé

里肌肉……………………110公克
金針菇……………………70公克
香菇…………………………3朵
① ｛ 鹽、味精、太白粉…各少許
　　高湯……5杯
② ｛ 鹽………1小匙
　　味精……½小匙

110 g. (4 oz.)　pork loin
70 g. (2½ oz.)　golden mushrooms
3　　　　　　dried black mushrooms
① dash each　salt, corn starch
② ｛ 5 C.　stock
　　 1 t.　salt

❶ 金針菇洗淨去頭，以開水略燙備用；香菇泡軟去蒂切絲備用；里肌肉切絲入①料略醃備用。
❷ ②料煮開，入香菇、肉絲及金針菇再煮開即可。

❶ Wash the golden mushrooms and trim off the end; boil slightly to use. Soak the dried black mushrooms with warm water to soften; discard the stem and shred. Shred the pork and marinate in ①.
❷ Bring ② to a boil, add mushrooms, pork, and golden mushrooms. Bring to a boil again and serve.

銀絲湯（圖右上 illus. right up）
Soup of Silver Threads

❶ 將冬粉泡軟切小段，金針菇洗淨去頭，乾金針泡軟洗淨備用。
❷ 將①料煮開，入洋蔥絲、金針菇、金針煮約2－3分鐘，再入冬粉及肉絲，待煮開後撒上蔥花及麻油即可。

❶ Soak bean thread in warm water and cut into shorter sections. Wash the golden mushrooms and cut off the end. Soften the dried lily buds in warm water, trim off the tough end, then wash.
❷ Bring ① to a boil, add onion, golden mushrooms, and dry lily buds; boil for 2 to 3 minutes. Then add in bean thread and pork; bring to boil again. Sprinkle green onion and sesame oil before serving.

冬粉‥‥‥‥‥1½捲(90公克)
里肌肉絲‥‥‥‥80公克
金針菇‥‥‥‥‥60公克
乾金針‥‥‥‥‥30公克
洋蔥絲‥‥‥‥‥½杯
蔥末‥‥‥‥‥‥1大匙
麻油‥‥‥‥‥‥少許
①{ 高湯‥‥‥‥5杯
　　鹽‥‥‥‥‥1小匙
　　味精‥‥‥‥¼小匙
　　胡椒粉‥‥‥少許

90 g. (3 oz.)　　bean thread
80 g. (2³/₄ oz.)　shredded pork loin
60 g. (2 oz.)　　golden mushrooms
30 g. (1 oz.)　　dried lily buds
½ C.　　　　　shredded onion
1 T.　　　　　green onion
Dash　　　　　sesame oil
①{ 5 C.　stock
　　1 t.　salt
　　dash　pepper

蘿蔔絲蛤蜊湯（圖右下 illus. right down）
Turnip and Clam Soup

❶ 蘿蔔絲及①料煮約20分鐘，再入蛤蜊及薑絲煮開，撒上蔥末即可。

■ 蛤蜊買回來後要先泡水吐沙。（參考第8頁）

❶ Cook turnip and ① for 20 minutes over medium heat. Add clams (see page 8 for preparing clams) and ginger, bring them to a boil; sprinkle green onion on the soup and serve.

蛤蜊‥‥‥‥‥‥600公克
蘿蔔絲‥‥‥‥‥2杯
薑絲、蔥末‥‥‥各2大匙
①{ 高湯‥‥‥‥4杯
　　鹽‥‥‥‥‥1小匙
　　味精‥‥‥‥½小匙

600 g. (1¹/₃ 1b.)　clams
2 c.　　　　　shredded turnip
2 T. each　　shredded ginger,
　　　　　　　minced green onion
①{ 4 c.　stock
　　1 t.　salt

6人份 Serves 6

翠綠竹筍湯（圖左 illus. left）
Refreshing Bamboo Soup

❶ 竹筍切滾刀塊；排骨切3公分塊狀，入開水川燙備用。
❷ 將竹筍、排骨及水5杯煮開，再改小火煮約30分鐘，起鍋前加九層塔及①料即可。

竹筍(淨重)……250公克
排骨……………150公克
水………………5杯
九層塔…………少許
① { 鹽…………½小匙
　 { 味精………¼小匙

250 g. (8³/₄ oz.) bamboo shoot
150 g. (¹/₃ 1b.) pork ribs
5 C.　　　　　 water
few sprigs　　 sweet basil
¹/₂ t.　　　　　 salt

❶ Cut bamboo shoot lengthwise into slanting pieces; cut pork ribs into 3 cm (1¹/₃") cubes, parboil the ribs to use.
❷ Bring bamboo shoot, pork, and water to boil; reduce to low heat and simmer for 30 minutes. Sprinkle sweet basil and salt before serving.

蕃茄牛肉湯 (圖右上 illus. right up)
Chinese Style Bortsch Soup

牛腩⋯⋯⋯⋯⋯480公克
蕃茄⋯⋯⋯⋯⋯240公克
水⋯⋯⋯⋯⋯⋯12杯
葱末⋯⋯⋯⋯⋯1大匙

①
```
葱段⋯⋯⋯⋯6段
薑片⋯⋯⋯⋯3片
八角⋯⋯⋯⋯1個
酒⋯⋯⋯⋯⋯4大匙
紅辣椒片⋯⋯1大匙
```

②
```
鹽⋯⋯⋯⋯⋯1¼小匙
糖⋯⋯⋯⋯⋯¾小匙
麻油⋯⋯⋯⋯少許
```

❶ 牛腩切塊，入開水川燙，撈出洗淨；蕃茄洗淨去蒂切塊。
❷ 牛腩、蕃茄、①料及水煮開，改小火燉1½小時(汁約剩一半)，加②料並撈出葱、薑、紅辣椒、八角，起鍋前撒上葱末即可。

❶ Parboil cubed beef, drain and wash clean. Wash, discard the stem, and cube the tomato.
❷ Bring beef, tomato, ① and water to boil; reduce to low heat for 1 ½ hour (soup reduced to half), add in ② and discard green onion, ginger, hot red pepper, and star anise. Sprinkle minced green onion and serve.

480 g. (1 1b. 1 oz.) beef brisket
240 g. (8½ oz.) tomato
12 C. water
1 T. minced green onion

①
```
6 sections  green onion
3 slices  ginger
1  star anise
4 T.  cooking wine
1 T.  sliced hot red pepper
```

②
```
1¼ t.  salt
¾ t.  sugar
Dash  sesame oil
```

翡翠白玉湯 (圖右下 illus. right down)
Soup of Green and White Jades

魚丸⋯⋯⋯⋯⋯300公克(約12個)
豆苗⋯⋯⋯⋯⋯250公克

①
```
高湯⋯⋯⋯⋯4杯
麻油⋯⋯⋯⋯1小匙
鹽⋯⋯⋯⋯⋯⅔小匙
胡椒粉⋯⋯⋯少許
```

❶ 豆苗去老纖維，洗淨備用。
❷ ①料煮開後入魚丸再煮開，待魚丸浮起隨入豆苗即可。

❶ Snip off the old fiber of the green peapod tip; wash the tender leaves and stems to use.
❷ Bring ① to boil, add in fish balls; bring to boil again. When all the fish balls are floating on top, add in the green peapod tip. Serve hot.

300 g. (⅔ 1b.) fish balls
250 g. (8¾ oz.) green peapod tip

①
```
4 C.  stock
1 t.  sesame oil
⅔ t.  salt
dash  pepper
```

八珍瓜丁湯
Soup With Eight Treasures

❶ 雞胸肉、里肌肉、火腿均切小丁，再以開水燙過備用；冬瓜切小丁；香菇泡軟去蒂切小丁；干貝加水蒸軟撕成細絲備用。
❷ 燉盅內入1項材料及①料，以大火蒸1小時即可。

❶ Dice the chicken breast and the pork; parboil and drain. Soak dried black mushrooms in warm water to soften; dice and cut of the stem. Steam the dried scallop in a little water until softened shred to use.
❷ Place ❶ and ① in a large soup bowl. Steam over high heat for an hour and serve.

冬瓜······300公克
雞胸肉、里肌肉······各50公克
火腿······25公克
香菇······3朶
干貝······1個
水······2大匙
① 高湯······4杯
酒······1大匙
鹽、薑末······¼小匙
味精······少許

300 g. (²/₃ 1b.)	diced winter melon
50 g. (1³/₄ oz.) each	chicken breast, pork loin
25 g. (1 oz.)	diced Chinese ham
3	dried black mushrooms
1	dried scallop
2 T.	water

① 4 C. stock
1 T. cooking wine
¼ t. each salt, minced ginger

罐頭玉米醬······1罐
絞肉、蝦仁、生蚵···各75公克
高湯······5杯
酒、鹽、太白粉······各少許
① 酒······1大匙
鹽······1小匙
味精······¼小匙
胡椒粉······少許
② 水、太白粉······各1大匙

1 can	cream of corn
75 g. (2²/₃ oz.) each	grounded pork, shelled shrimp, oyster
5 C.	stock
a little each	cooking wine, salt, corn starch

① 1 T. cooking wine
1 t. salt
dash pepper
② 1 T. each water, corn starch

6人份 Serves 6

三鮮玉米羹
Corn Porridge with Three Delicacie

❶ 蝦仁洗淨，生蚵以太白粉略抓洗，再沖水洗淨瀝乾備用(參見第5頁)。
❷ 絞肉、蝦仁、生蚵分別以少許酒、鹽及太白粉拌醃20分鐘備用。
❸ 高湯加玉米醬及①料煮開，入絞肉、蝦仁、生蚵再煮開，以②料勾芡即可。

❶ Wash and devein the shrimp. Toss oyster with corn starch (see page 5) and rinse clean; drain to use.
❷ Marinate pork, shrimp, and oyster individually with a little cooking wine, salt, and corn starch for 20 minutes.
❸ Bring stock, cream of corn and ① to boil, add in pork, shrimp, and oyster. Bring to a boil again, thicken with ② and serve.

酸辣海參絲
Spicy Sea Cucumber Soup

❶ 海參泡軟洗淨（參見第9頁）切絲，香菇泡軟去蒂切絲。
❷ ②料煮開，入①料煮沸片刻，最後以③料勾芡即可。

❶ Soak the sea cucumbers until softened (see page 9); wash and shred. Soak the dried black mushrooms in warm water until softened; cut off the stems and shred.
❷ Bring ② to a boil, add ① to boil again for a while. Thicken with ③ and serve.

海參……………………………2條
香菇……………………………6朵
①熟筍絲、火腿絲……………各⅓杯
　高湯…………………………4杯
　白醋…………………………2大匙
　酒、黑醋…………………各1大匙
②醬油…………………………2小匙
　鹽、糖………………………各1小匙
　味精、麻油、胡椒粉……各少許
③水、太白粉…………………各3大匙

2	sea cucumbers
6	dried black mushrooms

① ⅓ C. each cooked and shredded bamboo shoot, shredded ham

	4 C.	stock
	2 T.	white vinegar
	1 T. each	cooking wine, black vinegar
②	2 t.	soy sauce
	1 t. each	salt, sugar
	few drops	sesame oil
	dash	pepper
③	3 T. each	water, corn starch

6人份 Serves 6

6人份 Serves 6

蛤蜊雞湯
Chicken Broth With Clam

❶ 雞腿洗淨剁塊,入開水中川燙去血水；竹筍切滾刀塊；蛤蜊洗淨，泡水吐沙(參考第8頁)備用。
❷ 將雞塊與綠竹筍及①料入大碗中，放入蒸籠裏以大火蒸40分鐘後，續入蛤蜊及薑絲，再蒸10分鐘即可。

❶ Wash and cube the chicken legs;parboil to rid the blood, so the soup will be clear. Cut the bamboo shoot lengthwise into slanting pieces. Wash and sand the clam (see page 8) to use.
❷ Place the chicken, bamboo shoot, and ① in a large bowl, steam over high heat for 40 minutes; add clam and ginger, steam for another 10 minutes. Serve hot.

雞腿…………………2隻(約400公克)
綠竹筍(淨重)………300公克
蛤蜊…………………150公克
薑絲…………………1大匙
　水……………………4杯
　酒……………………1大匙
①鹽……………………⅔小匙
　味精…………………¼小匙

400 g. (14 oz.)	chicken legs
300 g. (⅔ lb.)	bamboo shoot
150 g. (⅓ lb.)	clams
1 T.	shredded ginger

	4 C.	water
①	1 T.	cooking wine
	⅔ t.	salt

長春湯
Soup of Eternal Youth

6人份 Serves 6

豆腐皮‥‥‥‥‥‥1½張
高湯‥‥‥‥‥‥‥4杯
蒜苗‥‥‥‥‥‥‥2隻
蛋‥‥‥‥‥‥‥‥1個
① { 絞肉‥‥‥‥‥120公克
    蝦仁‥‥‥‥‥75公克
    絞肥豬肉‥‥‥20公克
    葱末‥‥‥‥‥½大匙
② { 太白粉‥‥‥‥1小匙
    鹽‥‥‥‥‥‥¼小匙
    味精‥‥‥‥‥少許
③ { 鹽‥‥‥‥‥‥¾小匙
    味精‥‥‥‥‥½小匙

1½ sheet   bean curd sheet
4 C.   stock
2 stalks   garlic leek
1   egg
    120 g. (4⅓ oz.)   grounded pork
    75 g. (2⅔ oz.)   peeled shrimp
① { 20 g. (⅔ oz.)   grounded pork
                      fat
    ½ T.   minced green
                      onion
② { 1 t.   corn starch
    ¼ t.   salt
    ¾ t.   salt

❶ 將每張豆腐皮切成8小張的三角形(圖1)，共12小張；蛋打散；蒜苗切斜段均備用。
❷ ①、②料混合拌勻成餡，分成12等份，以豆皮包成餛飩狀(圖2)備用。
❸ 高湯煮開後入❷項材料、③料，並徐徐加入蛋液，最後撒上蒜苗即可。

❶ Cut bean curd sheet into 8 small triangles (illus. 1), 12 in total. Beat the egg; cut garlic leeks into slanting sections.
❷ Mix ①, ② thoroughly into filling; separate into 12 equal parts. Put the fillings onto each piece of bean curd sheet and fold it into wonton shapes (illus. 2).
❸ Bring the stock to a boil, add in ❷. and salt, then slowly pour in beatened egg. Sprinkle garlic leeks on top and serve.

八寶豆腐羹
Bean Curd Soup with Eight Treasures

豆腐·················1塊
雞胸肉··············150公克
蛋白·················1個
太白粉··············1½大匙
　青豆仁、熟筍丁、玉米粒、洋火腿丁
　·················各150公克
　香菇丁········5公克
　水·················4杯
　鹽·················1½小匙
　味精··············¾小匙
　胡椒粉···········少許
　水、太白粉······各1½大匙

	bean curd
150 g. (⅓ 1b.)	chicken breast
	egg white
½ T.	corn starch
150 g. each	green pea, corn starch
	cooked and diced
	bamboo shoot,
	diced ham
5 g.	diced black mushroom
4 C.	water
1½ t.	salt
Dash	pepper
1½ each	water, corn starch

❶ 豆腐以濾網磨細(圖1)，入½個蛋白及1大匙太白粉拌勻備用。
❷ 雞胸肉剁碎，入½個蛋白及½大匙太白粉拌勻即為雞泥(圖2)備用。
❸ ②料煮開，入豆腐及雞泥煮開，加①料再煮開，以③料勾芡即可。

❶ Strain the bean curd through a sieve (illus. 1); add in ½ egg white and 1 T. corn starch. Mix thoroughly.
❷ Minced the chicken, add in ½ egg white and ½ corn starch. Mix thoroughly.
❸ Bring ② to boil, add in bean curd and chicken. Bring to boil again after adding ①. Thicken with ③ and serve.

酸辣湯
Hot and Sour Soup

6人份 Serves 6

里肌肉‥‥‥‥‥‥‥‥‥‥‥75公克
蛋‥‥‥‥‥‥‥‥‥‥‥‥‥‥2個
① { 筍絲、木耳絲(圖1)、豆
腐絲、紅蘿蔔絲‥‥‥‥‥各⅓杯
② { 醬油、太白粉‥‥‥‥‥各1小匙
麻油‥‥‥‥‥‥‥‥‥‥½小匙
③ { 醋‥‥‥‥‥‥‥‥‥‥‥3大匙
葱絲、薑絲、醬油‥‥‥各2大匙
香菜‥‥‥‥‥‥‥‥‥‥1大匙
麻油、胡椒粉‥‥‥‥‥各1小匙
④ { 高湯‥‥‥‥‥‥‥‥‥‥4杯
鹽‥‥‥‥‥‥‥‥‥‥‥1小匙
糖‥‥‥‥‥‥‥‥‥‥‥½小匙
味精‥‥‥‥‥‥‥‥‥‥少許
⑤水、太白粉‥‥‥‥‥‥‥各3大匙

75 g. (2²/₃ oz.) pork loin
2   eggs
① {
   ¹/₃ C. each
      shredded bamboo shoot
      shredded black wood ear
      shredded bean curd
      shredded carrot
② { 1 t. each soy sauce, corn starch
    ¹/₂ t.   sesame oil
③ {
    3 T.   vinegar
    2 T. each soy sauce
               shredded green onion
               shredded ginger
    1 T.   coriander
    1 t. each sesame oil, pepper
④ {
    4 C. stock
    1 t. salt
    ¹/₂ t. sugar
⑤ 3 T. each water, corn starch

❶ 里肌肉切絲入②料略醃，蛋打散備用；③料置大湯碗中備用。
❷ ④料煮沸後入①料及肉絲，煮至肉絲熟再以⑤料勾芡，徐徐加入蛋液，最後盛入備有③料之湯碗中即可。

❶ Shred the pork loin and marinate in ② for a while. Beat the egg to use. Place ③ in a large soup bowl to use.
❷ Bring ④ to a boil, add in ① and pork. When the pork is done, thicken with ⑤; then slowly pour in the egg in long streaks. Pour the soup in the large soup bowl with ③ and serve.

❶

豆腐丸子湯
Bean Curd Ball Soup

豆腐、里肌肉…………各150公克
小白菜…………………75公克
筍片……………………30公克
木耳片、紅蘿蔔片……各20公克
高湯……………………5杯

① ⎰ 蛋白………………1個
  ⎰ 太白粉……………1小匙
  ⎰ 鹽…………………½小匙
  ⎰ 味精………………¼小匙
  ⎱ 胡椒粉……………少許

② ⎰ 鹽…………………1小匙
  ⎱ 味精、麻油………各¼小匙

150 g. (⅓ lb.) each bean curd,
                     pork loin
75 g. (2⅔ oz.)   baby cabbages
30 g. (1 oz.)   sliced bamboo
                     shoot
20 g. (⅔ oz.) each   sliced carrot
5 C.   stock

① ⎰ 1   egg white
  ⎰ 1 t.   corn starch
  ⎰ ½ t.   salt
  ⎱ dash   pepper

② ⎰ 1 t.   salt
  ⎱ ¼ t.   sesame oil

❶ 豆腐用篩網過濾成豆腐泥備用；小白菜去根部洗淨切3公分長段備用。
❷ 里肌肉去白筋，剁成肉泥，加①料拌勻，用力甩打至有黏性，再與豆腐泥充分攪拌備用。
❸ 水6杯燒開，先關火，用手將❷項材料擠成丸子狀(圖1)入鍋中，待全部擠完再開小火，煮至丸子浮起，撈出備用。
❹ 高湯加筍、木耳、紅蘿蔔煮熟，再入丸子、小白菜及②料即可。

❶ Press bean curd through a sieve to bean curd mash. Wash baby cabbages and discard the roots, cut into 3 cm (1⅓") long sections.
❷ Remove the white sinews of the pork; mince fine to mash. Mix with ① well; beat until sticky. Add in bean curd and mix thoroughly.
❸ Bring 6 C. of water to boil. Turn off the heat. Squeeze ❷ into small balls (illus. 1) and add into the water. Cook with low heat after all balls are in the water. Simmer until all balls are floating on top. Lift the balls out.
❹ Boil bamboo shoot, black wood ear, and carrot in the stock until done; add the balls, baby cabbage, ② and serve.

青江肉丸湯
Green River Meat Ball Soup

青江菜·················225公克
雞胸肉·················180公克
肥豬肉·················75公克
荸薺···················3個
蛋白···················1個
香菇···················6朵

① {
酒、太白粉······各1小匙
麻油···············½小匙
鹽···············3／8小匙
味精···············¼小匙
胡椒粉···········1/8小匙
}

② {
鹽···············¾小匙
麻油···············½小匙
味精···············¼小匙
}

225 g. (8 oz.)	bok choy	
180 g. (6⅓ oz.)	chicken breast	
75 g. (2⅔ oz.)	pork fat	
3	water chestnuts	
1	egg white	
6	dried black mushrooms	

① {
1 t. each cooking wine, corn starch
½ t. sesame oil
3/8 t. salt
1/8 t. pepper
}

② {
¾ t. salt
½ t. sesame oil
}

❶ 雞胸肉、肥豬肉及荸薺剁碎,再加蛋白及①料用打均勻備用。
❷ 香菇洗淨泡軟去蒂(圖1);青江菜洗淨,去子葉部份(圖2),切適當大小備用。
❸ 水5杯煮開,入香菇稍煮,再將雞泥擠成丸子狀,入湯中煮至丸子浮起,起鍋前入青江菜及②料再煮開即可。

❶ Mince chicken, pork, and water chestnuts; add in egg white. Beat in ① thoroughly.
❷ Soften the black mushrooms with warm water and discard the stems (illus. 1); wash the bok choy and remove the leaves (illus. 2), cut into desired sizes.
❸ Bring 5 C. of water to boil, add in black mushrooms. Form the chicken mixture into small meat balls; add into the soup. Cook until the meat balls float on top of the soup. Add in bok choy and ②, bring to boil again before serving.

這是給他的！

這是給她的？

親愛的阿傑：

謝謝你的禮物，我很喜歡它。

P.S. 晚上早一點回來，我做你最喜歡吃的！

美惠：

今天不是什麼特別的日子，我卻要送你一份特別的禮物。

老公阿傑 敬奉

P.S. 它不貴，卻代表我的一點心意！

味全

消費者服務中心0080-221007

味全文化教育基金會，以促進家庭幸福、創造和樂社會爲宗旨。自民國68年成立以來，致力於幸福家庭系列活動之推展，成效卓著，獲教育部及台北市政府評選爲推展社會福利最佳社團。味全文教基金會將永續傳承，作爲推動和諧社會的動力。

Wei-Chuan Cultural Educational Foundation   aims to promote family happiness and create harmony in society. Since establishment in 1979, it has pursued in developing activities concerning family happiness with great success;and was awarded by the Education Ministry and Taipei City Government as the best community service organization. Wei- Chuan Cultural Educational Foundation will continue its fine tradition to give impetus to promote harmony of society.

味全文化教育基金會

地址：台北市松江路125號5 F

電話：508- 4331・506-3564

Wei-Chuan Cultural Educational Foundation

Add : 5th Fl., 125, Sung-Chiang Rd. Taipei, Taiwan, R.O.C.

Tel : (02)508-4331・506-3564

味全家政班 開設有烹飪、插花、美姿、語文及兒童才藝等短期
進修班，30餘年來參加這些技藝研習的婦女兒童已達數十萬人。長年
累積的聲譽，使味全家政班揚名全球各地。

Wei-Chuan Cooking School not only offers cooking classes for
professionals and food lovers, but also provides short term courses for flower
arrangement, beauty care, etiquette, language. At the same time, offers many
successful after-school learning programs for children. Hundreds of thousands
of women and children have enrolled in these skill-training courses over the
past 30 years. Through years of accumulated good reputation, Wei-Chuan is
now known all over the world.

味全家政班
地址：台北市松江路125號5 F
電話：508-4331・506-3564

Wei-Chuan Cooking School
Add : 5th Fl., 125, Sung-Chiang Rd. Taipei, Taiwan, R.O.C.
Tel : (02)508-4331・506-3564

味全

低塩、甘脆
吃不膩！
LESS SALT、CRUNCHY
WITH A TASTE
THAT NEVER TIRES.

味全上口罐頭系列
wei-chuan shang-ko can foods series.